" Besides being beautiful little hand-sized objects themselves, showcasing exceptional writing, the wonder of these books is that they exist at all . . . Uniformly excellent, engaging, thought-provoking, and informative."

Jennifer Bort Yacovissi,
Washington Independent Review of Books

" . . . edifying and entertaining . . . perfect for slipping in a pocket and pulling out when life is on hold."

Sarah Murdoch, *Toronto Star*

" . . . a truly terrific series of meditative reads."

Megan Volpert, *PopMatters*

" Though short, at roughly 25,000 words apiece, these books are anything but slight."

Marina Benjamin, *New Statesman*

OBJECT LESSONS

A book series about the hidden lives of ordinary things.

Series Editors:

Ian Bogost and Christopher Schaberg

Advisory Board:

Sara Ahmed, Jane Bennett, Jeffrey Jerome Cohen, Johanna Drucker, Raiford Guins, Graham Harman, renée hoogland, Pam Houston, Eileen Joy, Douglas Kahn, Daniel Miller, Esther Milne, Timothy Morton, Kathleen Stewart, Nigel Thrift, Rob Walker, Michele White.

In association with

Georgia Tech | **Center for Media Studies**

BOOKS IN THE SERIES

potato

REBECCA EARLE

BLOOMSBURY ACADEMIC
NEW YORK • LONDON • OXFORD • NEW DELHI • SYDNEY

BLOOMSBURY ACADEMIC
Bloomsbury Publishing Inc
1385 Broadway, New York, NY 10018, USA
50 Bedford Square, London, WC1B 3DP, UK

BLOOMSBURY, BLOOMSBURY ACADEMIC and the Diana logo
are trademarks of Bloomsbury Publishing Plc

First published in the United States of America 2019

Cover design: Alice Marwick

A catalog record for this book is available from the Library of Congress.

ISBN: PB: 978-1-5013-4431-2
ePDF: 978-1-5013-4433-6
eBook: 978-1-5013-4432-9

Series: Object Lessons

Typeset by Deanta Global Publishing Services, Chennai, India
Printed and bound in the United States of America

To find out more about our authors and books visit www.bloomsbury.com
and sign up for our newsletters.

This book is dedicated to Susan, and the memory of Clifford Earle

CONTENTS

INTRODUCTION: LYING AROUND LIKE A LATKE

Sometime in 2015 the Irish artist Kevin Abosch sold a photograph of a potato for €1,000,000. Leaving to one side the question of how a black-and-white image of an organic potato could be worth that much money, what possessed Abosch, known for his penetrating portraits of public figures such as the activist Malala Yousafzai or the artist Yoko Ono, to photograph a potato in the first place?

According to Abosch, potatoes are our close cousins. 'I see commonalities between humans and potatoes that speak to our relationship as individuals within a collective species', he commented shortly after the sale.[1] Abosch has a knack for photographing people in ways that focus attention on their individuality, their quiddity, while at the same time forging a connection to the viewer. For Abosch, potatoes too offer an opportunity to connect. 'I use the potato as a proxy for the ontological study of the human experience', he explained – if this gnomic remark can be called an explanation.

FIGURE 1 Kevin Abosch, *Potato 345*, 2010. The Irish artist Kevin Abosch has photographed a number of potatoes, some in their birthday suits, still covered with the earth from which they emerged, and others adorned with festive gilt. Potatoes, according to Abosch, tell us something about the human condition. Potato 345, shown here, is at once a modest new potato, a living planet suspended against the night sky, and the subject of one of the world's most expensive photographs. Studio Kevin Abosch.

Potato 345, in its monumental framing of a single new potato and its astonishing price-tag, takes us by surprise because we rarely think of potatoes in grandiose terms. Most of the time, potatoes are a byword for ordinary. They are a staple. They are dependable and trustworthy. 'She's a real potato', you say in Norwegian, when someone is totally reliable, or at least that's what a Norwegian told me. They are stolid, a bit sedentary; couch potatoes that they are, they lack get-up-and-go. When your Jewish grandmother says, 'Don't just lie around like a latke', or potato pancake, she means 'Get off your backside and do something'. And everyone understands what Karl Marx meant when he compared the peasantry to a sack of potatoes.[2]

All over the world potatoes are an everyday food. 'We eat lots of them.' People from many different places told me this when I mentioned that I was writing about potatoes. 'Where are potatoes actually from?' was another common response. These days the correct answer would be: 'everywhere'. China is the world's largest producer, and the greatest potato-eaters are Belarusians (189 kilos per person per year), trailed by Russians (136 kilos) and Ukrainians (131 kilos). At present there are some 4,500 classified varieties of cultivated potato, along with nearly 200 wild species. According to the United Nations, there is not a single country in the world where potatoes are not grown, if we exclude the five for which we have no data. Because we eat so many potatoes, they are fourth on the list of the world's most important food crops.[3]

We don't think of potatoes as exotic. Quite the opposite; they are utterly familiar. When he was growing up in 1970s India the artist Subodh Gupta wondered whether everyone ate potatoes, or if it was only people in Bihar. A French traveller visiting Colombia in the early nineteenth century was surprised to see 'European' potatoes sold alongside South American vegetables such as cassava.[4] For an Indian boy potatoes are Indian. For a Frenchman they are European. This is pretty remarkable for a food that was totally unknown to most of humanity before the sixteenth century. Until then the only people who ate potatoes lived along the spine of mountains that runs from the Andes in Bolivia and Chile northwards through the Rockies. These mountains are the origin, the *omphalos* of potatoes. No one else had laid eyes on a potato before Spanish conquistadors arrived in South America in the 1530s and set about overthrowing the Inca empire. That set in motion a whirlwind that blew potatoes to India, Australia, upstate New York, and beyond. This makes it all the more extra-ordinary just how ordinary potatoes are these days. Their very names proclaim their rootedness in the right-here, in exactly wherever we are: Jersey royals, Idaho russet, Irish cobbler, Darjeeling red round. Even the Incas viewed the potato as pretty ordinary. An Andean legend from long before the Spanish arrived tells of the 'Baked Potato Gleaner', a mythical beggar who encapsulated the tuber's underdog status.

What *can* a potato tell us about the nature of human experience? Let's look at Abosch's *Potato 345*.

Potato 345 is a planet, an asteroid, the whole world. Stark against the dark night sky, it is rich with organic life, with brown earth. A growing tangle of roots marks a small forest, or perhaps the path of a river. We could live on this planet.

It is also a body, a human body, even. Delicate thread-like hairs emerge from its flesh, intimate strands growing out of dark, thick patches of earth clinging to its skin, revealing a living, generative fecundity. A small dimple suggests a belly button, an *ombligo* in Spanish, an umbilicus. The word umbilicus comes from the Greek *omphalos*, a stone that marks the centre of the world. It connotes fertility, life, and power. Beneath the potato's *omphalos*, a V-shaped parting suggests access to its mysterious interior.

Potato 345, floating against the inky cosmos, recalls the equally fecund body of the little limestone figure found near the Austrian village of Willendorf in the early twentieth century. During excavations at an archaeological site in 1908 a workman unearthed a small statue of a woman. The figurine, naked aside from her small knitted hat, dates from the Palaeolithic era, and now resides in Vienna's Natural History Museum. Traces of earthy red ochre are still visible around her deep belly button and other crevasses. Round as a potato, she lies silhouetted against the velvet backdrop of her storage case, mysterious and ancient. We don't know what the so-called Venus of Willendorf represents, but her ample body promises life, nourishment and, perhaps, a point of origin.[5] No ancient myth relates that all humanity emerged from a cosmic potato, but this is what *Potato 345*, together with the Woman of Willendorf, suggest to me. Abosch's potato is at once a planet, the world, and a living, fecund human body, still covered with the earth from which it emerged. It is a point of origin.

What stories lie behind the potato? This book tells several, about the potato's role in the emergence of modernity, and its power to channel our yearning to connect to the universe, and each other. The potato is entangled with the birth of the liberal state and the idea that the individual, rather than the community, should form the basic building

FIGURE 2 *Woman of Willendorf*, c. 25,000 BCE. This little limestone figurine was unearthed in Austria in 1908. Her generous proportions suggest fecundity and abundance. Her rounded form and earthy colouring bring to mind Abosch's *Potato 345*; both are vibrant with the promise of new life. Together, they remind us of our origins. Naturhistorisches Museum Wien.

block of society. It is also a source of quiet comfort and communion, a reminder of our rootedness in the here-and-how. Like Abosch, I see 'commonalities between humans and potatoes that speak to our relationship as individuals within a collective species'. Thinking about potatoes turns out to be a good way of thinking about some of the important tensions in our world, between individual choice and public benefit, between freedom and well-being, between despair and hope. Another title for this book might be: *Potatoes, or the Pursuit of Happiness*.

1 POTATO MOTHER

Omphalos

'Those times when we grew gold, pure gold ...'[1]

All 4,500 named varieties of potatoes trace their ancestry to the Americas. Wild potatoes grow along the American cordillera, the mountains that run from the Andes to Alaska. People living on its slopes have been eating potatoes for time out of mind. Stone tools and preserved potato peels show that wild potatoes were being prepared for food in southern Utah and southcentral Chile nearly thirteen thousand years ago; similar evidence dates their domestication from at least 7,800 BCE on the northern coast of Peru.[2] They formed an important part of the diet of many of the cultures inhabiting the nine thousand kilometres between Utah and Chile. Together with foods such as quinoa and maize, they provided a robust, starchy backbone to cuisines also enriched with chile peppers, beans and other vegetables. Each variety can be propagated from a 'mother potato'. She sounds like an ancient deity but in botany the term refers to the mundane tuber or seed potato that provides the genetic material from which additional plants are cultivated.

One difficulty with potatoes is that they are difficult to store. Anyone who has ever lost track of a bag of potatoes knows this. They have an unfortunate tendency to send forth a tangle of roots, and, worse, rot into a foul-smelling puddle. Andean peoples solved this problem by freeze-drying. Exposing potatoes to the intense cold of the high mountains transforms them into little fists of stone, immune to decay. The technique also neutralizes the poisonous glycoalkaloids present in some of the bitter varieties, allowing these to be eaten safely. If the potato-rocks are trampled underfoot like petrified grapes, it is possible to reduce them to a dry powder that lasts for years. This dried substance, *chuño*, captivated Spaniards when they first encountered it in the sixteenth century, and they invariably described in some detail how it is made. Europeans were however slow in adopting it themselves; it was left to industrial manufacturers in the twentieth century to bring us Smash and other commercially produced instant mashed potatoes.

Because potatoes were an essential part of the daily diet in the Andean world, their cultivation was a matter of importance. Various rituals helped ensure an abundant harvest. One account from sixteenth-century Peru describes the festivities that marked the inauguration of the planting season in the mountain village of Lampa. Local dignitaries seated themselves on carpets to watch the proceedings. A procession of richly attired attendants accompanied the seed potatoes, which were carried by six men making music on drums. Events culminated with the sacrifice of a particularly beautiful llama, whose blood was immediately sprinkled on the potatoes. Comparable practices (not necessarily involving llama blood) persist to the present day. Spanish priests objected strongly to these ceremonies but were often powerless to prevent them.[3]

The Andean writer Felipe de Guaman Poma de Ayala described the agricultural potato cycle in an extraordinary manuscript that he composed in the early seventeenth century, after the arrival of Europeans. The son of indigenous nobility, Guaman Poma was born shortly after the Spanish conquest of his homeland. Late in his life he was moved to recount the history that he had to some extent witnessed first-hand. Guaman Poma's *New Chronicle*, as he titled the thousand-page text, offered a universal history of the world, from Adam and Eve, through the Inca monarchs, to the dismal period of Spanish rule, whose multiple evils Guaman Poma documented in detail.[4] It also described the ritual calendars of both Christian and Incaic religions, and the agricultural tasks carried out each month. The chronicle is illustrated lavishly with Guaman Poma's idiosyncratic and immensely appealing line drawings. Several show the labour required to cultivate the essential potato. Digging sticks in hand, a man and woman weed the field in the picture for June, while a second woman ports a heavy sack away for storage. Other drawings depict men and women at work sowing seed potatoes and tending the abundant plants.

FIGURE 3 Felipe Guaman Poma de Ayala, *June: Time of Digging up the Potatoes*, 'El primer nueva corónica y buen gobierno', 1615–16. Potatoes were an essential foodstuff for Andean people. This seventeenth-century drawing by the self-taught Felipe Guaman Poma shows a potato harvest. By using digging sticks rather than ploughs farmers were able to cultivate very steep slopes, thereby making efficient use of the mountainous terrain. After the harvest some potatoes would have been freeze-dried so that they could be stored for a long time. GKS 2232 quarto, Det Kongelige Bibliotek, Copenhagen.

Unlike maize, which held a high status within the Inca state, potatoes were considered a lowly food, necessary but banal. Even in the potato's *omphalos* they were viewed with some disdain. Along the Andes, maize was used to brew the all-important *chicha* or *aqha*, the corn beer that accompanied virtually every important political encounter. Potatoes played no comparable role in high diplomacy; for Andeans as for us, they were ordinary things. Guamon Poma contrasted the robust stature of maize eaters with puffy, effete villagers forced to subsist on dried *chuño*.

For these reasons, potatoes did not enjoy the intense state ritual lavished on the maize crop. The Inca himself participated every year in a symbolic maize-planting ceremony, to the accompaniment of music and song. Similar state-level festivities marked the maize harvest, and the intervening period was overseen by a team of priests who fasted throughout the planting season and kept track of the crop's progress. In the sacred fields around the Inca capital, Cuzco, small gold replica cornstalks were interspersed among the growing maize, to 'encourage' it.[5] No such imperial oversight was bestowed on potatoes. Cultivated a village level, they were traded and consumed within more local orbits, their growth fostered by smaller rituals such as the one that took place centuries ago in Lampa, where the sprinkling of llama blood on seed potatoes distressed the Catholic cleric.

All potatoes nonetheless benefitted from the attention of the Potato Mother, Axomama, daughter of the earth goddess Pachamama, and sister to Saramama, the Maize Mother. As these names suggest, Andean potato language and cosmology are rich in feminine reproductive power. Plant breeders, perhaps unwittingly, replicate this vocabulary when they speak of the mother tubers from which all potato plants derive. Watching over the potato fields in the Andes – which scientists suggestively call the tuber's 'cradle area' – Axomama cares for her tuberous offspring. Together with her sisters and their all-powerful mother, Axomama controls the earth's fertility, overseeing the growth of potatoes and other things necessary for sustenance. Household shrines to Pachamama and her fertile daughters balanced state-level neglect of potatoes. The veneration of this feminine dynasty long pre-dated the official rituals of the Inca empire, and persists to the present.

For Andean farmers, human history and human bodies were entangled with these plants and the broader universe. Beautiful or unusual potatoes were themselves miniature Potato Mothers, and all encapsulated the generative powers of the female body. 'Corn and clay, potatoes and gold were linked together as emblems of female powers of creation', writes the historian Irene Silverblatt.[6] Just as Abosch's Potato 345 is at once a solid, earthly potato, an organic, living planet, and perhaps a human body, so a Potato Mother is the fecund mother plant used to breed up new generations of potatoes, and an ancient being in command of the earth's powerful generative strength. Today Andean potato farmers coddle the skittish, feminine soil, hoping she'll feel sweet enough to favour them with a good harvest. In the happier days before colonialism, they recall, 'we grew gold, pure gold': potatoes as golden nuggets, living stones.[7]

The Moche, who lived along the northern coast of Peru in the first millennium CE, formed beautiful ceramic containers in the shape of potatoes. Moche potters often created realistic replicas of ordinary foodstuffs such as potatoes, or squash

FIGURE 4 *Moche Stirrup Vessel*, 100–800 CE. The Moche inhabited the northern coast of what is now Peru. They left behind many beautiful ceramic vessels, some depicting people, plants and animals, often with striking realism. The skilled ceramicist who shaped this container arrayed the four potatoes so that they point to the four cardinal directions of the universe. The pot is at once a realistic portrayal of an important Andean food, and an acknowledgement that agriculture, nourishment and life itself unfold within a larger cosmology. Museo Larco, Lima, Peru.

or maize. At the same time as they represented the elements of the mundane kitchen world these clay recreations alluded to the overarching spiritual universe that made all existence possible. In the vessel shown in Figure 4, the four potatoes point to the four corners of the universe.[8]

Alongside such lovely earthenware vegetables Moche potters crafted disturbing vessels that meld human faces disfigured by cuts and slashes, missing lips and noses, with the form of a potato. A strange, bulbous figure looks back at us from the pot in Figure 5, its body formed from lumpy tubers. Three eyes stare out from its belly. Lacking lips, it can only grimace with its unnaturally wide mouth.

Redcliffe Salaman, the author of a monumental history of the potato first published in 1949, developed the theory that these pots depict the unfortunate victims of Andean harvest rituals. Some people, he surmised, were selected to represent the potato harvest. The more 'eyes' a potato develops, the more shoots it sends out, which means it will produce more prolifically. Perhaps, in order to ensure a bountiful crop, these symbolic potato-people had additional eyes incised into their own bodies, or their lips excised to widen their mouths into another huge eye. Living Mr Potato Heads, their faces became potatoes – people and potatoes superimposed to reveal their unexpected commonalities. Anthropologists have questioned this interpretation, but that's what I think of when viewing these strange pots. They remind us that the story connecting humans to potatoes is a tale of violence as well as sustenance.

FIGURE 5 *Moche Vessel of a Potato with Anthropomorphized Head*, 6–600 CE. Three bulbous tubers make up the body of an unhappy-looking creature with too many eyes and no proper mouth. What sort of being is this? The historian Redcliffe Salaman surmised that such vessels represent the people sacrificed to ensure a good potato harvest. Perhaps, he speculated, these victims had extra 'eyes' etched into their living faces, to encourage the seed potatoes to send forth many shoots. By excising their lips their mouths could be widened artificially into another sprouting eye, converting their bodies into symbolic potatoes. Ethnologisches Museum–Staatliche Museen zu Berlin, Stiftung Preußischer Kulturbesitz, and Claudia Obrocki (photographer).

The great hunger

'And where potato diggers are you still smell the running sore.'[9]

In Ireland the connections between potatoes, people, sustenance and suffering run deep. The Great Famine of 1845 to 1848, which resulted in the death or emigration of a fifth of the population, marked Irish history. Potatoes arrived in Ireland in the sixteenth century, probably from Spain, and over the next centuries came to play an ever more important role in the diet of the Irish poor. The potato's superlative power to convert earth and light into calories made it possible for entire families to live on the minute patches of land onto which the rural Irish were squeezed as commercial wheat, dairy and meat production expanded after the English colonized Ireland in the sixteenth century. By the 1840s some forty per cent of the population subsisted almost entirely on potatoes, or potatoes with a bit of buttermilk if they possessed enough land to pasture a milch cow. Poor men in rural Ireland ate between three and five kilos of potatoes a day and little else.[10] The varieties grown were as limited as this diet. While a single valley in the Andes might contain over a hundred different types of cultivated potato, most of the potatoes grown in nineteenth-century Ireland were a yellow-fleshed variety known as Irish Lumper. Monocultures are extremely vulnerable to disease, since a single pathogen can devastate the entire harvest. When Ireland's potato crop failed in 1845, and again in 1846 and 1848, over a million people died.

The Famine was triggered by an outbreak of late blight (*phytophthera infestans*), a micro-organism probably originating in the Americas, but the magnitude of the calamity was greatly increased by the response of the British government, which viewed the crisis as a welcome opportunity to reshape Irish society. In the opinion of officials such as Charles Trevelyan, chief administrator at the Treasury in London, Ireland's entire economic structure was an affront to modern capitalist practice. Because it was possible (just) to live off them, potatoes allowed rural Irish families to evade the discipline of wage labour by remaining self-sufficient. The collapse of the potato economy would, he hoped, propel Irish smallholders off their tiny plots of land and into the ranks of the proletariat. This, Trevelyan believed, would an enormous improvement, well worth the 'transient evil' of famine. It would also sweep away the inefficient and listless class of Irish landlords, whom the British held responsible for the catastrophic humanitarian crisis. The last thing the British government should do, from his perspective, was prop up this archaic system with aid to the stricken Irish. For liberals such as Trevelyan, the potato was an obstacle to modernity, a roadblock on the march towards economic rationality. It was the enemy of the state.

'What hope is there for a nation which lives on potatoes?', he exclaimed in disgust.[11]

Trevelyan's view that the potato was responsible for the immiseration of the Irish peasant was widely shared. It was this history, more than anything, that prompted the potato historian Redcliffe Salaman to declare the potato 'the most perfect instrument for the maintenance of poverty and degradation'.[12] Potatoes, fulminated the nineteenth-century social agitator William Cobbett, were a damnable crop because they kept the Irish alive to be exploited by landlords. They were the root 'of slovenliness, filth, misery, and slavery'.[13] They reduced men to the state of animals, or, actually, potatoes. In Cobbett's opinion, Irish peasants had become virtually indistinguishable from the potatoes they lived off. The miserable, dirty hovels in which the Irish sheltered differed little from underground potato beds. The lumpen Irish peasant and the Lumper potato were virtually one and the same.[14] 'Commonalities between humans and potatoes' indeed.

But in Ireland the potato is not a signifier only of death, and the cruel mercies of Trevelyan's brave new world of waged labour. It is also a symbol of nourishment, of sustenance, of the bonds that link families together, of Axomama and her sustaining offspring. The great Irish poet Seamus Heaney captured both aspects of the potato. Born in 1939, Heaney grew up on a small farm in Northern Ireland. The rhythms of rural life shaped his poetry, as did Ireland's folkways and its troubled history. Heaney alluded to all of these influences in the lecture delivered in 1995 when he accepted the Nobel Prize for Literature.[15]

Heaney's much-lauded poetry captures the potato's complex resonance in Ireland. In his poems, potatoes signal his own past, connecting him to his parents and grandparents. Preparing potatoes with his mother, watching his father dig a potato bed, become re-enactments of his own lineage, his own rootedness in Irish history, as well as reminders of his sometimes-uncomfortable relationship with that past. Peeling potatoes in silence with his mother was, he declared in a 1987 sonnet, the closest bond they ever shared, a cold comfort to recall after her death. Potatoes in Heaney's poetry transmit the steady rhythm of the everyday. A basket of new potatoes counterbalances the gashes carved in Irish society by political violence. In 'After a Killing', the sight of a young girl shopping for vegetables hints that, like it or not, life will continue despite the omnipresence of death.[16] Equally powerfully, potatoes bespeak the painful history of the Famine.

'At a Potato Digging' (1966) evokes the Famine, and also the potato's inescapable centrality to life itself.[17] The poem is shaped by a constant elision between people and potatoes. It begins with a description of a modern harvest. Despite the century that has passed since Black '45, the first year of the Famine, its shadow looms over the exhausted workers, who in stooping down to gather in the potatoes, bow in homage to the dark earth, the 'black Mother' of potatoes and of life and death:

> Centuries
> Of fear and homage to the famine god
> Toughen the muscles behind their humbled knees,
> Make a seasonal altar of the sod.

No nourishing Axomama this hard deity.

The second stanza describes the living, pulsing potatoes themselves. The newly harvested potatoes are slippery, damp newborns nurtured by their black Earth Mother, who

> erupts
> knots of potatoes (a clean birth)
> whose solid feel, whose wet inside
> promises taste of ground and root.

Like subterranean rabbits the fecund potatoes mature in a 'hutch of clay' under the earth. Just as the Moche perhaps incised potato eyes into living human faces, Heaney makes the potatoes into human heads. They are 'live skulls, blind eyed', sightless but animate. After the harvest they lie stored in long clay pits that are all too resonate of human graves. Potatoes and people alike are born from the dark earth and return to it.

The tomb-like storage pits presage the Famine, when 'stinking potatoes fouled the land'. The new potatoes, once 'sound as stone', have rotted in their clay burial place. Reversing the image of the potato as a living skull, the starving Irish become themselves 'live skulls, blind eyed'.

'Wild higgledy skeletons', they are pecked to death by hunger as the potatoes lie dead in the 'bitch earth' who has refused to nourish her people. The final stanza returns to the present, as the resting harvesters, 'dead-beat' but at least alive, spill 'libations of cold tea, scatter crusts' on the black and faithless earth, still propitiating their fickle mother with these offerings. The poem unites past and present, people and potatoes, all dependant on the fertile but unreliable body of the earth herself. Heaney's black earth Mother, like Axomama, links the potato to the mysterious reproductive powers of women's bodies, and indeed to all human bodies.

Heaney's poetry speaks to the commonalities between people and potatoes noted by Kevin Abosch. It seems fitting that Irish poet and Irish potato have both been the objects of Abosch's photography. Abosch's portrait of Heaney was made in the same year as his photograph of Potato 345. Each appears silhouetted against a starless black sky, complete and undeniable in their individuality.

Father potato

The resonance between families, history and the mundane world of the potato is evoked with equal power in the work of another poet whom Heaney admired: the Chilean Pablo Neruda. Heaney shared with Neruda a commitment to poetry that explored the everyday, functional objects that populate our lives. Like Heaney, Neruda valued 'the used surfaces of things, the wear that hands give to things'. His poems consistently honoured both worn surfaces and the nameless workers whose lives he sought to resurrect.[18]

Neruda's childhood was precarious; his father barely eked out a living as a railwayman and his son's ambitions to write poetry enraged him. A poet Neruda nonetheless became, winning fame and admiration first for his unabashed celebration of sexual desire in *Twenty Love Poems and a Song of Despair*, and later for his ability to condense into poetry an entire universe of natural beauty, human struggle, the dignity of labour, and the transcendence of love. Like Heaney, he was awarded a Nobel Prize for Literature.

In the 1950s Neruda began work on a series of poems that he called 'elementary odes'. Neruda had recently joined the Chilean Communist Party, formalizing a long-standing inclination. In keeping with his newly affirmed political convictions, he began experimenting with less grandiose forms of poetry, which would reflect the material reality of life, rather than exploring metaphysics and the aesthetic avant garde. The elementary odes were the result. Many of them focus specifically on the vigour and authenticity of working-class culture. As one critic put it, they elevate 'the commonplace and the everyday to the dignity of poetic treatment'.[19] They were written in the midst of personal turmoil; Neruda's wife had recently learned of his affair with Matilde Urrutia, a Chilean singer who had been hired to care for him when he fell ill during a stay in Mexico. The odes are nonetheless mostly joyful in tone, celebrating the mundane pleasures of everyday life. Food is a recurrent theme; Neruda wrote odes to onions, tomatoes, olive oil ('the celestial key to mayonnaise'), and bread, as well as potatoes. All are praised as simple, honest foods eaten by ordinary people.[20]

While Heaney cursed the potato as a bitch mother, and Andean potato farmers honoured the potato mother, Neruda hailed the potato as a father. 'Ode to the Potato' opens with a declaration of the poet's lineage: he is the native son of the Chilean potato.[21] Playing off the similarity of the South American terms for potato (*papa*) and father (*papá*), Neruda insists on calling the potato *papa* rather than *patata*, as it is known in Spain. 'Potato, I call you 'potato-father' and not *patata*', he proclaimed. The ode sets out explicitly the shared heritage that links Neruda to the honest, New World potato. Addressing the potato, the poet explains that 'you were not born a pure Spaniard, you are dark like our skin. We are Americans, potato-father, we are Indians'. Neruda and the potato are members of the same South American family. Later stanzas explain how their common mother carefully planted her potatoes in a soft, moist nest in the earth, where they sheltered, little treasures, the true wealth of the Indies. When hordes of acquisitive conquistadors ravaged the land, they found not golden goblets, but potatoes, a different sort of bounty.

Praising the potato as the 'enemy of hunger', honoured by all nations, Neruda's ode celebrates its quiet modesty. Our potato-father is content to rest honourably in the earth, anticipating no great fanfare. 'You are not expecting my song, because you are deaf and blind, and buried', Neruda admitted, before musing whether the hot oil of a frying pan might provoke the potato to break its silence. Potatoes for Neruda, as for Heaney, are our close relatives, and their suffering is our suffering.

Ill with prostate cancer, Neruda died in 1973, twelve days after the military coup that brought Augusto Pinochet to power. It is probable that he was murdered on the orders of the new regime, which despised his political views and his poetry.[22] Shortly afterwards Neruda's friend, the poet Yevgeny Yevtushenko, composed an 'Epistle to Neruda' to honour his passing. It concludes:

> But today I see Neruda—
> he's always right in the centre
>   and, not faltering,
> he carries his poetry to the people
> as simply and calmly
>   as a loaf of bread.[23]

Or a potato, Yevtushenko might have written.

2 GLOBAL CITIZENS

Immigrant roots

In 2016, shortly after 51.9 per cent of Britons voted to leave the European Union, posters started to appear in British cities announcing that 'Potatoes Are Immigrants'. A cheerful heap of chips, together with one of those little takeaway forks, completes the image.

At a moment when the nation's immigration policies were under intense scrutiny, the posters questioned the assumptions behind the hostility to migrants by suggesting that even the most British of foods was itself, originally, an immigrant. Versions of the poster were spotted in the United States shortly afterwards. The image was designed by Mia Frostner and Rosalie Schweiker. 'We were trying to come up with something funny that would explain how there is no such thing as British or monoculture', Schweiker commented.[1] Potatoes do that perfectly. They are the quintessential immigrant, arriving without fanfare, performing useful functions, and attracting little attention, at least at first. In most cases they travelled without documents, which makes it

FIGURE 6 Mia Frostner and Rosalie Schweiker, *Potatoes Are Immigrants*, 2016. Versions of this poster appeared across the United Kingdom in the weeks following the 2016 vote in favour of Brexit. The pile of takeaway chips depicts one of the UK's most typical late-night snacks. Chips are essentially British, but the potatoes from which they are made originated far away, on the other side of the Atlantic. With great economy the poster reminds viewers that most cultures are built on migration and exchange. Keep It Complex and Mia Frostner.

challenging to trace their movements. We know that in 1615 the Mughal statesman Asaf Khan served 'potatoes excellently well dressed' at a banquet in Rajasthan, but we have little clue as to how they got there, all the way from the Andes.[2]

But what exactly is a potato? That's not a straightforward question. Botanists explain that the 'ordinary', 'Irish', or 'white' potato, *Solanum tuberosum*, is entirely distinct from the sweet potato (*Ipomoea batatas*), another a native to the Americas. It also differs from other new-world tubers such as the Jerusalem artichoke (*Helianthus tuberosus*) or cassava (*Manihot esculenta*). 'White' potatoes are members of the *Solanacea* family, together with tomatoes, chile peppers and aubergines. Sweet potatoes are related to bindweed, the irritating garden pest, but are only distant relatives of the ordinary potato. Jerusalem artichokes and cassava are different genera altogether.[3]

Yet why let the botanists decide? All these plants originated in the Americas, and all travelled around the world as part of the 'Columbian exchange', the worldwide transfer of plants and animals begun in 1492 with Columbus's arrival in the West Indies.[4] There are therefore many reasons to view their histories as deeply interconnected. To the people first encountering these roots in Rajasthan, Vienna or the Canary Islands, they were all members of the same unfamiliar clan more notable for their similarities than for their differences. Naturally they sometimes shared their passports with each other, or confused immigration officials on arrival.

In the confusion the paperwork, where there was paperwork, became muddled. Names were modified or transformed entirely in the global Ellis Island that is language. In Spain potatoes are today called *patatas*, while sweet potatoes are *batatas*, both of which derive from Spanish efforts to reproduce the word Taino people in the Caribbean used to label sweet potatoes. Jerusalem artichokes are the very similar *patacas*. Their shared names tell us that the family resemblance between all three roots overrode any botanical distinction. The same semantic linkage explains the English terms 'potato' and 'sweet potato', although the English at first called sweet potatoes *Spanish* potatoes, because they came to England via Spain. In Spanish America, potatoes are still *papas*, the Quechua term used in the Andes, and source of Pablo Neruda's playful pun with the word for papa. (For what it's worth, Jerusalem artichokes are so-called not because they were associated with the holy city, but because they are related to the sunflower. These cheerful flowers not only resemble bright, crayoned suns, but also turn to face their namesake. Pass a field of sunflowers and you'll see them all pointing in the same direction. Their Italian name, *girasole* – 'turn-towards-the-sun' – proclaims this tendency even more clearly. 'Jerusalem' is in English less of an alien mouthful than *girasole*; as to their surname, they do taste a little like the globe artichoke, if you think about it.)

Other early European names for these new arrivals underlined their essentially rooty character. 'Roots', *raíces*, is what the first Spanish accounts call potatoes.[5] Sixteenth-century German writers employed a range of overlapping terms, all of which located these tubers where they belong, under the ground: *Griblingsbaum*, from *gruben*, to dig; *Erdäpffeln* or *Erd Artischocken* (earth apples or artichokes); *Tartuffeln* (truffles) and simply *Knollen*, or roots. Many of these terms (or variations thereof) now refer unambiguously to the potato; an entertaining chart in a linguistic atlas maps the dozens of names used today for the potato across German-speaking lands.[6] Given our poor knowledge of their individual itineraries, however, we can't always be certain whether a sixteenth-century German writer meant a potato, a sweet potato, or something else when he said he'd tried a new type of root called an earth apple.

Other European languages too described the potato as an underground apple, or pear. Scandinavian writers referred to 'jordpäron' (earth-pears), 'jordäpple' (earth-apples), and 'peruvianska nattskatta' (Peruvian nightshade), as well as 'potatoës'. In today's French it's a *pomme de terre*. The link to truffles dates back to the earliest Spanish descriptions and was common in a number of European languages. The sixteenth-century Flemish botanist Carolus Clusius and his network of fellow naturalists referred, in multiple languages, to 'taratonfli', 'tartufy', 'papas americanorum', 'papos', and 'papes'. Writing from Padua, the botanist Gian Vincenzo Pinelli for instance asked Clusius for a sample of these 'roots which one eats like truffles'.[7] Some of the earliest French descriptions similarly refer to 'tartoufles' or 'cartoufles' – this, incidentally, is probably the origin of another German word for potato, *Kartoffel*.[8]

Scholars who wish to sort out the paperwork associated with the individual itineraries that took potatoes, sweet potatoes and their tuberous relatives to Europe and beyond have a difficult task. But it's worth recalling that imprecise names are not simply errors, or lamentable sources of tiresome linguistic confusion. If early modern writers failed to differentiate clearly between these different vegetables, this tells us that they perceived them as similar. These overlapping names reveal something about the reception of these plants, in the same way that the multiple terms for maize used in central Africa provide some of the few clues to the early history of that plant's spread across the continent.[9]

Fortunately for those of us interested in potatoes, even the most discreet traveller sometimes leaves behind traces of their passage. Recipes are one place we can begin to find evidence for the potato's journey from the Andes to everywhere.

The earliest known recipe for what might be a potato dates from 1581; it appears in a cookbook written by Max Rumpolt. He was the personal chef for the Archbishop-Elector of Mainz. Born in Hungary, Rumpolt was an experienced cook who had worked for a number of noble houses before taking the position in Mainz. His cookbook offered thousands of recipes as well as over thirty sample menus and advice on shopping and table etiquette. The work is enlivened by woodcuts by Jost Amman, a Swiss artist who specialized in book illustrations.

Alongside its recipes for a Hungarian tart with many layers and instructions on how to craft sugar into the shape of an entire Parmesan cheese or a castle, *Ein new Kochbuch* included recipes for a number of American novelties from kidney beans to, alarmingly, a beaver, which Amman depicted in a jaunty woodcut. Since Rumpolt was familiar with these New-World foods, it's not implausible that he had also encountered potatoes, sweet potatoes and the other new American roots. It's likely that he learned about all these new foods via some unknown Spanish connection, since the book contained recipes for quite a few Spanish dishes such as an 'Holepotrida', or *olla podrida*, the most iconic early modern Spanish dish, an elaborate stew in this case to be prepared with a New-World turkey (also illustrated by Amman).

Ein new Kochbuch includes several recipes for what Rumpolt called 'earth-apples'. It's not entirely clear what these are. Today *Erdapfel* is one of the German words for potato. Perhaps Rumpolt was referring to the potato or perhaps a sweet potato, or something else entirely. I think it's a potato. If it was, then it's the first written recipe for potatoes in existence. In any event, he instructs readers to 'Peel and cut them small. Parboil them in water and press well in a fine cloth. Chop them small and roast in bacon cut into little pieces. Add a little milk and let cook together. This way it is tasty and good'.[10] Certainly that is a sensible way to prepare potatoes.

A decade after Rumpolt's earth-apple recipe, another German, Wilhelm IV von Hessen, described how Italians prepared a new food called 'taratouphli' (roughly, 'truffles'), which they first boiled, and then peeled and dressed with butter; French cookbooks from the same years also explained how to prepare these new 'tartoufles'.[11] From England, the 1596 *Good Huswife's Jewell* offered a recipe for 'a tart that is a courage to a man or woman'. More like a pudding than a pie, the tart was a rich dish that included butter, eggs, spices and 'the braynes of three or four cocke-sparrows' alongside a 'potaton'.[12] Whether this was a potato, or some other new-world tuber, is again unclear, but elaborate potato pies and puddings remained popular for centuries. By 1611 Spanish cookbooks were criticizing such potato tarts as gastronomic monstrosities to be avoided at all costs – good advice, since in 1624 Richard Sackville, third earl of Dorset, died while gobbling up 'a potato pie'.[13]

By the early seventeenth century quite a few recipes explained to the curious (and literate) cook how to use a new sort of food called an earth-apple, or a truffle, or a potaton. A century later there were too many recipes for us to count, both from Europe and farther afield. The fashion of sweetened potato-meat pies lived on. From Boston Sarah Fayerweather, the wife of a wealthy merchant, recorded her version of 'patatoe pye' in her handwritten recipe book:

Boil ye patatoes well slice ym pound some mace & cinnamon fine, mix the spice wth ¼ lb of white sugar, strew it well over ye potatoes, yn take a pound of fresh butter cut it in slices put a layer of butter at ye bottom than a layer of patatoes, yn put over a layer of sweet meats, & a layer of marrow, & yn a layer of sweetmeats & marrow & a layer of butter on yr top.[14]

She recommended serving this rich assemblage with a sweet wine custard. French manuals explained how to make elaborate potato rissoles. More simply, Portuguese cookery books advised accompanying boiled potatoes with butter and mustard; alternatively, jaded diners could be amused by 'artificial potatoes' fashioned out of marzipan and dressed with melted butter.[15]

These early modern cookbooks offer snapshots of the potato's travels. Like a holiday photograph, they highlight unusual or especially memorable moments. No one was eating artificial potatoes as a daily staple. Cookery books less frequently capture the more mundane aspects of travel – the buses and hitched rides, the overnight stays in hostels – that underpin most travel. To understand those aspects of the potato's global journey we need to turn to other sources. Diaries, letters, tax records and court cases help us fill in some of the gaps.

Together these show that from the sixteenth century potatoes travelled around the world in the wake of European voyages of conquest, enslavement and trade. Captain Bligh, of *Bounty* fame, planted some in Tasmania in 1777, and by 1817 the island was able to export nearly 400 tons to Australia.[16] Although potatoes were known in Utah twelve millennia ago, it was probably English settlers who introduced them to the east coast of North America, where they were grown by Haudenosaunee (or Iroquois) farmers in upstate New York and Anglican ministers in Maine. By the eighteenth century they were a common food. A soldier fighting in the Adirondacks during the Seven Years' War noted in his diary that he had 'Con Clued the Day' with 'purtaters for Sup'.[17]

The potato was growing in Iran around 1800, according to British diplomats, who bickered among themselves over which of them deserved the credit for introducing it.[18] British colonial officials likewise claimed to have brought potatoes to Sumatra.[19] The colonial Agricultural and Horticultural Society of India, formed in 1820 to effect the 'general amelioration of the agricultural condition of India', made a sustained effort to encourage cultivation of 'this salutary and useful root', at the same time as they rubbished local agricultural practices. The potato had however made its own way to the subcontinent many years earlier through routes that we have yet to uncover.[20]

In most cases the agents of these transfers remain anonymous, the unrecognized transporters of undocumented immigrants. The historian Douglas Hall believed that the reason the early modern movements of plants are so difficult to reconstruct is that their agents were often themselves ordinary people below the sight lines of contemporary writers.[21] In general neither these people nor the plants they transported were of much interest to the individuals most likely to keep records. A central role must have been played by sailors, whose mobile lifestyle made them well-suited to spreading cultures, and cultivars, across oceans. It seems likely for example that it was Galician fishermen who first brought the potato to Ireland sometime in the late sixteenth century. Not only were mariners the probable initiators of a momentous transformation in the Irish diet; they were also fashion trendsetters, but that is another story.[22]

Kitchen pioneers

Histories of food often claim that for hundreds of years no one in Europe wanted to eat potatoes. The reasons offered seem ludicrous, and depressingly resonant of today's anti-immigration rhetoric, with its insistence on the profound cultural differences that supposedly separate Europeans from unwanted outsiders: apparently, potatoes were considered un-Christian because they are not mentioned in the Bible; or ordinary people were suspicious of the unfamiliar agricultural practices required to cultivate a tuber; or else potatoes were peculiar and lumpy and so might spread leprosy. ... This line of analysis is summed up in a recent study that blames 'the conservatism of the peasants' for the slow speed with which, allegedly, new foods such as the potato were adopted in Europe.[23] Ordinary Europeans, it seems, were not very welcoming to these new arrivals.

In fact, none of these stories hold water. Cabbages aren't mentioned in the Bible, but that proved no impediment to their consumption across Christendom, and anyone who's grown carrots knows they can produce strange, tumorous growths to rival anything a potato can offer. Early modern Europeans were not daunted by the need to cultivate potatoes from mother tubers rather than from seed; they were doing more or less the same thing with tulip bulbs in Holland in the same years, in fact.[24] Potatoes indeed took a long time to become a major commercial crop cultivated in open fields, but this does not mean that they did not find a home in cottage gardens alongside the equally unbiblical cabbage and other humble household vegetables.

All the evidence suggests that peasants and labourers were the first, not the last, to eat these new roots. In 1588 a gentleman in the Belgian town of Tournai proudly took a visitor on a tour of his botanical garden, to display his collection of rare and unusual flora. On seeing that the garden included some potato plants the visitor asked what they were doing in a botanical garden, since they were widely grown in Italy. The visitor reported that 'he had seen great abundance of them in Italy and that some people ate them in place of rape-roots, others cooked these bulbs with lamb, and others use them to fatten pigs, each according to his imagination'. Rape-roots, a kind of turnip, were the food of the poor. Italian peasants, who were quick to begin using maize in place of millet to make the now-iconic polenta, were apparently no less speedy in growing and eating potatoes. A cookbook from the mid-seventeenth century noted that in Germany these roots had become so common that they were grown in practically every cottage garden; the author therefore felt no need to explain how to prepare and cook them. It was likewise Polish peasants, not Polish noblemen, who first began to grow potatoes in their gardens.[25] The Bible's silence on the subject of potatoes was evidently no deterrent.

Disputes between tenants and clergy over how much of the harvest the church could legally claim in tithes also highlight the presence of potatoes in cottage gardens. Tithes were an ecclesiastical tax levied on agricultural produce by both Catholic and Protestant churches. Because the titheable status of a crop depended in part on whether it was intended for sale or personal use, litigation over potato tithes frequently delved into who was cultivating the potatoes and to what end. Cases from Spain and Belgium to as far afield as French Canada provide evidence that in many parts of Europe (and its colonial hinterland) potatoes were popular with ordinary labourers, who resented handing over part of their harvest sufficiently to go to court. When the rector in the Cornish parish of St. Buryan demanded that his tenants begin paying a tithe on their potatoes, they refused, insisting that they had been cultivating potatoes for their own use for 'for time out of mind', and that no one had ever tried to demand a tithe before. Dr Nicholas Boscawen was simply the first clergyman to pay attention to what they were up to.[26] Contrary to claims that 'the conservatism of peasants' impeded the potato's European travels, peasants and small farmers were the first to welcome these immigrants to their tables.

It should surprise no one that peasants and villagers were in the vanguard of agricultural and culinary innovation in early modern Europe. Like the maize that peasants in the Veneto grew to make polenta, potatoes are 'state evading': crops that enable a degree of autonomy from taxation and control because they can be cultivated on marginal ground and form part of complex household provisioning systems that are difficult to measure and tax efficiently.[27] They don't so much fly under the radar of the state, as grow, often underground, beneath its very nose. Tithe disputes reveal that locals had usually been cultivating their potatoes for decades before they attracted the attention of church officials.

The notion that peasants are inherently conservative is contradicted by what we know about peasant agriculture. A substantial body of research has established that small farmers in many parts of the world are perfectly capable of innovative agricultural strategies when faced with new plants and new economic situations.[28] Peasant farmers in mid-twentieth-century Tanzania for instance consistently readjusted their farming practices 'in accordance with climate changes, new crops, and new markets', although both government officials and representatives of the World Bank regularly bemoaned their supposed conservatism and unwillingness to abandon traditional agricultural practices.[29] Peasant farmers are often experimentalists, engaging in observation, interpretation, field trials, evaluation and manipulation in order to identify and develop new cultivars and new methods of cultivation. They discuss their experiences with others in their locality, exchange seeds and techniques, and adapt their own practices in light of these conversations. Exactly this sort of constant evaluation and innovation is responsible for the remarkable diversity of potato varieties in the Andes, where small farmers draw on a vast body of practical agronomic knowledge to match particular seed potatoes to the soil and environmental requirements of specific pieces of land. It is only when such practices are viewed from the lofty vantage point of developmentalist agronomics that lively cultures of local experimentation are transformed into an obstructive 'traditional outlook and unwillingness to change'.[30]

Recognizing early modern peasant agriculture as a site of flexibility and innovation is not simply a matter of historical justice; it is also relevant for our future. Crop diversity is today identified as an essential component of both long-term environmental sustainability and global food security. This essential diversity relies on the expertise of the world's small farmers, who are often acknowledged to be the most important counterweight to the forces of highly homogenized large-scale commercial agriculture. Small farmers grow crops for many different purposes – some to sell at market, some because they are particularly tasty or suitable for specific dishes, others for use as gifts or to store as capital against future expenses. Different ends call for different varieties that possess the particular qualities needed for each purpose. In some cases, storage capacity is the most important, in others yield or flavour. This sort of agriculture thus values, and promotes, crop diversity. It is not typically characterized by inertia and the reflexive replication of past practice. The potato's history reminds us not to overlook the contributions of small-scale agriculture to the larger history of agronomic innovation and change. The hundreds of local potato varieties grown today by small farmers in the Andes may help feed us in the future.

Quietly and gradually, potatoes spread from the American Cordillera to Europe and beyond, finding a home first in cottage gardens, and then in open fields and market stalls. They did this without fanfare. No officials, other than vicars looking to collect a tithe, or customs officers, were particularly interested in them. No statesmen suggested that potatoes were an important component of ensuring food security. No one composed promotional texts celebrating the potato as a source of good health and national well-being.[31] Public-spirited physicians did not send recipes for potato soup to newspapers. All of these things, however, began to occur in the late eighteenth century.

3 THE STATE OF THE POTATO

Stone soup

In 1758 Thomas Turner tried a new soup. The son of a grocer, Turner ran a general store in the English village of East Hoathly from 1750 until his death in the 1790s. At the age of twenty-four he began to keep a diary in which he recorded financial transactions, local events, and, especially, what he ate. His diet, and even more his drinking, caused him concern. He regularly vowed to drink less and eat more vegetables. Filled with remorse by his repeated failure to stick to his own good intentions, he made rash promises to breakfast once a week on dry bread, and other equally punishing, and unrealized, commitments.

Potatoes were no novelty to Turner. Like many people in eighteenth-century Britain, he consumed them regularly. On 27 January 1758, however, ordinary potatoes became part of an extraordinary soup. That Friday Turner noted that his household 'dined on the remains of Wednesday and yesterday's dinners with the addition of a cheap kind of soup, the receipt for making of which I took out of *The Universal Magazine* for December as recommended (by James Stonhouse MD at Northampton) to all poor families as a very cheap and nourishing food'. Turner's soup contained potatoes, turnips, dried peas, oatmeal and a little beef or mutton. Turner pronounced it 'a very good, palatable, cheap, nourishing diet'. He was pleased enough with it that a month later he invited his friend Thomas Davy, a shoemaker, to dinner 'to taste our soup'.[1]

The eighteenth century was awash with recipes for potato soup. Unlike elegant potato vichyssoise, silky with leeks and enriched with cream, these eighteenth-century potato soups were no-nonsense combinations of potatoes, pulses and perhaps a bit of meat. They were more like the stone soup I read about as a child. Perhaps you know the folktale: someone promises to make a soup, but all they have is a stone.[2] Clever cajoling elicits all the necessary ingredients from the guests themselves. In the end the cook's only contribution is a single stone, which, they swear, imparts a mysterious, but crucial seasoning. Somehow, to the amazement of the diners, the cook appears to have conjured an entire meal out of an inedible rock. These eighteenth-century potato soups were likewise ways of magicking a meal out of nothing at all, out of a potato, an onion, a few turnips.

A potato is very like a stone. It seems appropriate that Turner's soup recipe was provided by a Dr Stonhouse. Subodh Gupta, the Indian artist who wondered if only people in Bihar ate potatoes, captured the potato's stone-like qualities in his 2013 *Food for Others*: eleven sleek, gleaming gilded potatoes nestle alongside two duller potatoes made of bronze. The gilded potatoes are more beautiful than the matt bronze ones, but none of them is edible. They're all stones, all equally unsuitable for making soup, or anything else.

Why did the aptly named Dr Stonhouse send the *Universal Magazine* his potato recipes in the first place? At the time, Sir James Stonhouse was a successful physician in Northampton, in central England, where he ran the local infirmary. Although in his youth he had been 'extremely licentious both in principles and practice', he later embraced the Anglican

FIGURE 7 Subodh Gupta, *Food for Others*, 2013. Thirteen bronze potatoes, eleven gold-plated, all inedible: Subodh Gupta's beautiful, stony potatoes are aptly designated as 'food for others'. During the eighteenth century, potatoes were the quintessential food for others. Hundreds of pamphlets, sermons and advertisements encouraged working people to eat more of them. Courtesy of the artist and Hauser & Wirth.

church, first publishing a series of religious pamphlets with titles like *Spiritual Directions for the Uninstructed*, and then taking religious orders.[3] His economical recipes doubtless reflected his Christian concern for Northampton's poor. They also formed part of a tidal wave of potato soups that swept over Europe during the Enlightenment. Recipes for potato soup were one element of a larger transformation in ideas about public health underway in the eighteenth century. While in previous centuries rulers had worried about the consequences of outright famine or acute shortage, statesmen had shown little interest in the everyday eating habits of ordinary people. The important thing was to avoid food riots. That changed in the Enlightenment: What ordinary people ate began to be a matter of political importance.

What a treasure is a potato garden!

Why were working people so feeble and sickly? Military officers and statesmen across eighteenth-century Europe asked themselves this question. A new appreciation of what we would now call public health emerged during the Enlightenment, as statesmen became increasingly convinced that national strength and economic prowess required more than a docile population disinclined to riot. They came to believe it required a healthy, energetic workforce of soldiers and labourers. This alone would ensure the success of industry, commerce and agriculture, and also defend the nation during the century's almost continual military conflicts. 'There is not a single politician', stated one writer, 'who does not accept the clear fact that the greatest possible number of law-abiding and hard-working men constitutes the happiness, strength and wealth of any state'.[4] Statesmen and philosophically minded individuals pondered how to build this population of healthy and vigorous workers. It was the productivity puzzle of the eighteenth century.

From the late sixteenth century treatises on good government had begun to suggest that states generally benefitted from a large population. A larger population provided a larger labour force for agriculture and industry and a wider pool of soldiers; these in turn would increase a prince's hold on power. This interest in the links between population size and state power encouraged the development over the next century of the mathematical skills, such as probability and statistics, necessary to measure population growth. By the eighteenth century, theorists of statecraft had come to view the population not simply as a personal resource of the prince, but as the bedrock of the wealth and power of the state. This conviction prompted a growing number of schemes aimed at protecting the population from disease and death through the draining of marshes, regulation of hospitals, and other public health measures. These ideas were commonplace in many parts of Europe by the mid-eighteenth century.[5]

A large population, however, was not in itself sufficient. A treatise on how to energise Spain's sluggish economy spelled out what more was necessary: the population needed to be usefully employed in some productive enterprise. As the treatise explained, 'when one says that a sovereign's wealth consists in the number of his vassals, one means the number of *useful* vassals, since a million idle vagabonds and professional beggars, far from being useful, are an impediment to the state, which would be much better off, and wealthier, without them'.[6]

In order to be diligent and useful a population needed to be healthy. Only then would a state be able to prosper. This in turn required not only inoculation schemes and programmes of marsh drainage, but also an adequate food supply. As the French chemist (and potato-promoter) Antoine-Augustin Parmentier observed, 'the type and choice of food greatly influences the population, so it is impossible to take too many precautions when ensuring that the people are well fed'.[7]

Most important, from this perspective, was ensuring an adequate supply of the sorts of foods suitable for the labouring body. When writers spoke of the need to ensure that the population was energetic and industrious, they had in mind the energy and industriousness of working people. The English philanthropist Jonas Hanway stated this plainly: 'the true foundations of riches and power is the number of working poor'.[8] National strength and wealth thus demanded, in the words of one of numerous pamphlets on the matter, that working people be 'plentifully and cheaply fed'.[9] The

FIGURE 8 Street sign for Avenue Parmentier, Paris, 2018. The French chemist Antoine-Augustine Parmentier was one of the eighteenth century's most renowned potato advocates. He published many essays on the potato's merits as a foodstuff, animal feed, and industrial product. Celebrated in his lifetime as a visionary humanitarian, he's now immortalized on French menus: *Parmentier* means a dish contains potatoes. Parisian street signs credit him with introducing the potato to France, which is a considerable overstatement. Parmentier worked to popularize the potato, but French people were eating it long before his efforts. Courtesy of Charles Walton.

interconnections between the bodies of working people, national prowess and a flourishing economy prompted an altogether new interest in the political implications of day-to-day eating practices.

How, however, to ensure that working people ate suitably nourishing foods? A profound transformation of the economic order to channel more wealth to the poor was out of the question for all but the most radical political philosophers. Instead, attention focused on identifying inexpensive alternatives to existing dietaries. Writing from Bologna, whose population had only recently recovered from losses in the previous century caused by outbreaks of plague, the agronomist and landowner Pietro Maria Bignami explained that were his homeland to possess an adequate food supply, its population would increase markedly – and if the population grew, industry would be sure to follow. Were that to happen, the region would undoubtedly become 'one of the richest and happiest in all Italy'.[10] To accomplish this, he believed it was necessary to identify 'a new product' able to compensate at least in part for the inadequacy of existing foodstuffs. Perhaps, he suggested, the potato might serve this purpose.

Bignami was not alone in hoping that the potato might address the need for a cheap, population-building staple for working people. All across Europe political thinkers pinned their hopes on the potato as a vehicle to deliver robust working populations. The renowned Scottish physician William Buchan argued this in several popular works. Buchan's career had included a stint as medical officer at an orphanage in Yorkshire, as well as in a private practice in London. These experiences informed his bestselling manual on household medicine, which explained how to treat earache, broken bones, and other misfortunes, alongside offering advice on the importance of clean clothing for students, the need for regular exercise, and much more. Buchan was dismissive of the eating habits of 'the poor', who in his view were largely responsible for their own ill health. In his opinion, 'peasants are extremely careless with respect to what they eat or drink, and often, through mere indolence, use unwholesome food, when they might, for the same expense, have that which is wholesome'. He also blamed sharp business practice by butchers and others for the unhealthy food that often featured on the tables of the poor. These matters, he stressed, should concern everyone, because spoiled food caused epidemic diseases, and also because 'the lives of the labouring poor are of great importance to the state'.[11]

Buchan expanded on these matters in his 1797 *Observations Concerning the Diet of the Common People*. Buchan's aim in both works was to show 'common people' how to live 'cheaper and better' by improving their diet.[12] Buchan reiterated that most 'common people' ate too much meat and white bread and drank far too much beer. They did not eat enough vegetables. The inevitable result, he stated, was ill health, with diseases such as scurvy wreaking havoc in the bodies of working men, women and children. This, in turn, undermined British trade and weakened the nation. Feeble soldiers did not provide a reliable bulwark against attack, and sickly workers did not enable flourishing commerce.

How, however, to ensure that soldiers and workers were sufficiently nourished? What sorts of food would provide a better nutritional base than beer and white bread? Buchan encouraged a diet based largely on whole grains and root vegetables, which he insisted were not only cheaper than the alternatives, but infinitely more healthful. He was particularly enthusiastic about potatoes. 'What a treasure is a milch cow and a potatoe garden, to a poor man with a large family!', he exclaimed. Farmers should make every effort to provide their labourers with such a garden. The potato, he stated, provided ideal nourishment. 'Some of the stoutest men we know, are brought up on milk and potatoes' – stoutness being a positive quality in a working man, indicative of general robustness and vigour. Buchan maintained that once people understood the advantages they would personally derive from a potato diet, they would happily, of their own free will, embrace the potato in place of white bread and beer. The benefits would accrue both to the individual workers and their families, whose healthy bodies would be full of vigour, and to the state and economy overall. Everyone would win. Simply enabling everyone to pursue their own self-interest would lead to a better-functioning body politic and a more productive economy, at least in Buchan's rosy imagination.

Buchan was one of a vast number of eighteenth-century potato enthusiasts. His views were absolutely typical of the hundreds of potato advocates scribbling away from St. Petersburg and Stockholm to Madrid. Local clubs in Finland sponsored competitions aimed at encouraging peasants to grow more potatoes. Spanish newspapers explained how to boil potatoes in the best Irish fashion. Monarchs across Europe issued edicts urging everyone to grow and eat more potatoes, and in 1794, in the apotheosis of potato fervour, the Tuileries Gardens in Paris were dug up and turned into a potato plot. And in case anyone wondered what to do with all those potatoes, every economical recipe detailed in Hannah More's 1795 *The Cottage Cook; or, Mrs. Jones's Cheap Dishes: Shewing the Way to do Much Good with Little Money* featured the tuber. Evidently, as one French writer remarked with surprise, the ordinary potato had become the darling of the Enlightenment.[13]

These potato fanciers never suggested, however, the people should be *obliged* to eat potatoes; rather, they explained, patiently, in pamphlets, public lectures, sermons and advertisements, that potatoes were a nourishing, healthy food that you, personally, would eat with enjoyment. There was no need to sacrifice one's own well-being in order to ensure the well-being of the nation as a whole, since potatoes were perfectly delicious. As the Italian physician Antonio Campini insisted in 1774, they provided 'good, healthy, agreeable and tasty nourishment'.[14] Individual choice and public benefit were in perfect and convenient harmony. Potatoes were good for you, and they were good for the body politic.

This is more or less the view of the United Nations Food and Agriculture Organization. Launching the 'Year of the Potato' in 2008, the FAO stated that

> the potato should be a major component in strategies aimed at providing nutritious food for the poor and hungry. It is ideally suited to places where land is limited and labour is abundant, conditions that characterize much of the developing world. The potato produces more nutritious food more quickly, on less land, and in harsher climates than any other major crop.

At the same time, as the FAO explained, 'we would not be celebrating the International Year of the Potato if potatoes weren't so good to eat!'. Their website offers a number of recipes, including four for soup.[15]

The FAO is absolutely correct that potatoes are an exceptionally efficient source of food energy. While a hectare of land sown with wheat might yield enough protein to feed seven people over the course of a year, a hectare of potatoes will nourish seventeen; only soybeans produce more protein per hectare, among the major crops. The contrast is even more striking as regards calories: a hectare of land will produce three times the calories if sown with potatoes compared to wheat or oats. Potatoes require less water than other crops, as well. A litre of water used in irrigation yields less than three calories' worth of rice, but more than twice the amount if the water is used to grow potatoes. Potatoes are in fact the best of all the important crops at converting water into calories.[16] The potato, in short, is an excellent way of feeding more people from the same agricultural inputs. It has further agricultural and nutritional merits, since it flourishes in a range of climates and growing conditions and is rich in vitamin C and other necessary nutrients.

For these reasons it's often been argued that the potato was at least in part responsible for the steady upward increase in the world's population, one of the most characteristic features of modernity. Since the sixteenth century, when the potato made its debut on the global stage, the world's population has grown from some 460 million to over seven billion. The causes of population growth are numerous and disputed, but there is considerable agreement that improved nutrition plays some role. This is not simply because access to better and more abundant food prevents people from starving. A better diet ensures greater resistance to disease, encourages fertility and also allows a person to be more energetic. Better-fed agricultural workers should be able to work harder, creating a virtuous circle of ever-increasing food supplies. The notion that potatoes fuelled modern population growth dates back to the nineteenth century and continues to attract support. A recent study concludes that potatoes account for an incredible 25 per cent of the world's total population increase.[17]

William Buchan, Antonio Campini, and the hundreds of other eighteenth-century potato enthusiasts were right to identify the tuber as an excellent source of nutrition, but the potato's nutritive qualities were not the reason why it assumed a celebrity status during the Enlightenment. After all, potatoes had been in Europe for over a century without officials showing the least interest in them. The reason why potatoes became politically visible was because the nature of statecraft had changed, in ways that accorded unprecedented importance on the diet of working people. As a result, this immigrant root acquired a new political relevance.

Anarchist tubers

The eighteenth-century apotheosis of the potato as a tool of statecraft represented a dramatic reversal in the tuber's political status, because hitherto it had functioned largely as an obstacle to state formation. For most of human history, rulers have not been very interested in foods that grow under the ground. Wheat, rice, and other above-ground cereals monopolized the attention of princes and officials. These crops are easy to notice, easy to store, relatively easy to transport, and for all these reasons easy to tax. The emergence of the world's earliest states is associated with the cultivation of grain. Priests, kings, elaborate military structures, and the taxation systems necessary to pay for them, first arose in areas that grew cereals.

Cultivating, harvesting and processing cereals such as wheat demands a good deal of labour, but the payoff is that they store well. Cereal-based cultures usually construct granaries to hold the crop once it has been harvested. The problem is that granaries are easy to spot: Passing groups of brigands, local strongmen and the state itself soon notice the presence of such stocks of grain; from spotting to stealing is a short step. The temptation to confiscate is all the more appealing since most of the work necessary to turn the plants into food – the cultivating, harvesting, threshing and drying – has already been done. All that the new owners need to do is grind, bake or boil their booty. It's been suggested that these risks motivated ancient grain-based communities to band together to form states to protect the harvest from bandits. Or perhaps, less benignly, the wealth derived from confiscating stores of cereal helped consolidate early states. In either case, the result was the emergence of ever-more-hierarchical social, political, religious and military structures, supported by taxation schemes levied at least in part on the very grains that had enabled their rise to power. Cereals help build states.[18]

In contrast, groups that cultivate tubers typically have less complex, and less hierarchical, social structures. Perhaps this reflects the specific features of subterranean crops such as potatoes or cassava. These roots don't need to be harvested at a precise moment, and they keep well if left in the soil; once dug up, however, they store poorly unless subjected to additional processing. For these reasons, communities subsisting on such foods have scant motivation to construct collective storage sites. As a result, they offer little for the outside world to confiscate. If the state wants your potatoes, writes the political anthropologist James C. Scott, it will have to 'dig them up tuber by tuber'. He argues that underground roots do not stimulate the growth of a state, with its attendant inequalities. If grain is a prerequisite for the formation of states, then perhaps potatoes are an obstacle. Scott refers to potatoes and their tuberous cousins as 'state evading', even 'state repelling'.[19] Scott's potato is an anarchist, opposed to hierarchy and structural inequality. In the view of nineteenth-century British officials, the potato played exactly this state-repelling role in Ireland, which is why they were so implacably opposed to the entire potato economy. Its eradication through the Famine, they hoped, would mark 'the commencement of a salutary revolution in the habits of a nation long singularly unfortunate' – namely their conversion into a rural proletariat.[20]

From the vantage point of the state, tuber-cultivating communities possess other characteristics that make them a further affront to orderly governance. They tend to move around, growing different crops in different zones, so it is difficult to monitor what they are up to. Their complicated agricultural practices make it difficult to calculate taxes, since it's rarely a matter of simply sending an official on a particular date to observe the size of the wheat harvest. States find such people, and their shifting, complex agriculture, annoyingly resistant to appropriation and control. Potatoes, seen in this light, are part of disruptive patterns of behaviour that prevent the state from visualizing the population and its doings.

William Petty reflected just this perspective in his assessment of the potato's impact on state formation. Born in England in the 1620s, Petty had an eventful life that took him to France and Holland, as well as Oxford and London, where he taught music and anatomy and helped found the Royal Society. In the 1650s he travelled to Ireland, which had recently been annexed by English forces under the leadership of Oliver Cromwell. Petty worked for many years as a representative of the English colonial state, which aimed to extract as much profit as possible from its new possession. He viewed the potato as a major obstacle to his plans to convert the recently-colonized Irish into a productive source of revenue for England. Because it was so easy to live on potatoes, the Irish did not work as hard as Petty would have liked, with the result that England was able to collect about half the taxes that Petty calculated a potato-free population would have yielded. Potatoes facilitated the Irish in lazing about, smoking tobacco, and generally resisting English efforts to convert them into sailors, labourers or other useful members of a commercial economy. In Petty's view the English state would have been considerably better off had the Irish eaten fewer potatoes.[21] Potatoes, for Petty, were firmly located on the wrong side of a gulf separating the modern world from backward, unproductive autarky.

In Ireland, the potato for centuries remained a thorn in the side of the British state, an anarchic Celt thumbing his nose at capitalist notions of wage labour and industriousness. Elsewhere writers such as William Buchan and Pietro Maria

Bignami hoped it would become a handmaiden of the modern state. Potatoes, it seems, are both cogs in the wheel of state formation, and a spanner in the works.

Happy potato family

I'm not sure how seriously to take the recipes in *How the Chinese Eat Potatoes*. One – for fried mashed potato sticks wrapped around garlic ramps – recommends serving the sticks with a spicy sauce and several live goldfish. What is clear is that the authors of this 2008 cookbook see the potato as an important component in China's overall development strategy: By eating more potatoes the Chinese can help address the challenge of a growing population. They will also improve their own health. In messianic tones reminiscent of eighteenth-century potato promoters, Dongyu Qu and Kaiyun Xie proclaim that the potato

is ideal as infant food due to its complete range of nutrients, abundant vitamins and soft texture. It has been reported that fresh mashed potatoes can be externally applied to heal bone fractures. Freshly extracted potato juice is very helpful in controlling several conditions, such as constipation, gastric ulcers, redundant acidity in the stomach, duodenum ulcers, and nasosinusitis. The potato is beneficial for cancer patients, especially for those undergoing chemotherapy, because of its tender fibers, high potassium, and several vitamins (namely vitamins A and B6). It is also regarded as an anti-senescence food because of its high vitamin C, E and B5 content, as well as its anthocyanin component, which can protect cells from attacks by free radicals.[22]

Who will not benefit from this miraculous food?

The Chinese government has been pushing potatoes for decades. China is now the world's leading producer of potatoes, growing some 22 per cent of the global crop, most of which are eaten in China itself.[23] Potatoes arrived in the seventeenth century but have long been viewed as a food of the poor. Grown on a village level, these politically uninteresting tubers allowed locals to evade the reach of the state. During the terrible famine that resulted from Mao's policies during the Great Leap Forward, when tens of millions of people starved to death, potatoes offered survival. The Chinese state requisitioned grain but not vegetables, and not potatoes. An oral history from the northern region of Beidahuang captures their importance in keeping body and soul together. Although Beidahuang as a whole suffered a shocking 18 per cent mortality rate (higher even than the Irish Famine), Feng, a peasant farmer, recalled that he and his village pulled through because 'there were so many potatoes'.[24] Grateful though survivors were, potatoes continue to be tarnished with famine memories. 'I grew up on potatoes' means 'My family was penniless'. Although potato consumption has increased markedly in the last decades, rice remains the core staple.

From the 1940s Chinese agronomists began to experiment with new, higher-yielding varieties and established programmes in potato breeding. By the 1960s there were about thirty research institutes working on potatoes, and leaders issued periodic commands that potato production be increased. As the Chinese state embraced the principles of a market economy, interest in the potato has grown markedly. The potato is now identified as an important component of China's overall food security. There are over a hundred institutes conducting potato research and commercial production has expanded dramatically.[25]

The connections between potatoes, political economy and a strong state explain the current Chinese government's interest in potatoes. Just as was the case in eighteenth-century Europe, this new Chinese potato promotion is motivated by concerns about the broader needs of a newly reconceptualized state. Equally reminiscent of the parallel process in eighteenth-century Europe, the recent Chinese potato promotion is framed in terms of individual choice and individual benefit. State television programmes disseminate recipes and encourage public discussion about the tastiest ways of preparing potato-based dishes, all as part of an effort to rebrand the potato as a healthful lifestyle choice.

The 'Happy Potato Family' campaign captures this perfectly. In one striking advertisement two cartoon potatoes, labelled 'Rich-Potato Brother' and 'Little Sister', cavort alongside a gaily dressed woman identified as 'Sister Potato'. The threesome smile cheerfully, undisturbed by

FIGURE 9 *The Happy Potato Family*, n.d. The Green Revolution of the 1960s transformed agriculture in China, as agronomists worked to popularize new varieties of rice; more recently the Chinese state has encouraged potatoes as a nourishing alternative to rice. This piece of propaganda associates potatoes with happiness and money: the caption puns off the similarities between the Mandarin words for *potato* and *bling*, to suggest that wealthy people eat potatoes. Image in the public domain.

their peculiar cross-species family. They form an unsettling modern counterpoint to Axomama and her Andean sisters.

'Sister Potato' is the *nom d'artiste* of Feng Xiaoyan, the woman in the patterned frock in the advert. Feng, a self-proclaimed peasant from the northern, potato-growing province of Shanxi, has attained national stardom through her enthusiastic promotional songs in praise of the potato. Appearing here alongside her cartoon siblings, she represents the ongoing effort to associate potatoes not with dutiful submission to state demands or dire hunger, but with personal wealth. The advert's caption is a pun on the currently fashionable term *tuhao*, which refers to the nouveau riche and happens to sound very similar to the word for potato. It translates roughly as 'Join us and let's all be rich-potatoes', or perhaps 'Come make some potato-bling with us'.[26]

As in eighteenth-century Europe, in today's China the idea is that everyone – you, the state, the population as a whole – benefits from these potato-eating campaigns. If everyone pursued their own self-interest, potato advocates past and present have argued, everyone would eat more potatoes, and then the population as a whole would be richer and healthier. Healthier people would be able to work harder. The economy would flourish, and the state would be stronger. Everyone would benefit, if only everyone followed their own individual dietary self-interest. These ideas endowed the act of eating dinner with a new political and economic significance. Today's healthy-eating plates and nutritional guidelines have their origins in these developments.

4 PLEASURE AND RESPONSIBILITY

Potatoes and the pursuit of happiness

'Happiness is regular sex and potatoes', reads a postcard on my desk. There *is* something very comforting about a potato. 'A well-boiled potato', the *Times* insisted in 1854, was the key to domestic harmony and marital happiness.[1]

Happiness was exactly what eighteenth-century potato promoters promised. The pursuit of happiness is, of course, a familiar slogan of the Enlightenment, enshrined perhaps most famously in the United States' Declaration of Independence. That it was the duty of the state to make its subjects happy was something on which virtually everyone agreed. Writers across Europe devoted immense energy to dissecting the nature and sources of happiness, whose pursuit on earth was, in the words of the historian Darrin McMahon, 'the great goal of the century'.[2] Potatoes, it turns out, were one way to achieve it, and at the same time build strong, competitive states.

Not just potatoes: potato soup. Thomas Turner's stone soup and its many relations were celebrated not only because they filled you up, but because they supposedly made you happy. This was the view of the inventor of the century's most famous potato soup: Benjamin Thompson, or Count Rumford. Born in Massachusetts in the 1750s, Thompson left North America in 1776, with the outbreak of the American Revolution. (Thompson was a loyalist.) After a spell working for the British military he served as an advisor to Karl Theodor, the elector of Bavaria. In Munich Thompson reorganized the Bavarian army and established what he called a 'House of Industry', a sort of internment camp for beggars and the indigent. The two enterprises were interconnected – interns at the workhouse at one point were set to work sewing military uniforms. Rumford said his aim was to 'make soldiers citizens, and citizens soldiers'. It was in recognition of these efforts that Karl Theodor awarded him the title of Count Rumford.[3]

A central element of this plan to transform Munich's poor into productive citizens was food. Food provided crucial energy, and it needed to be cheap. Rumford's experience running the Munich poorhouse provided him with ample opportunity to identify the 'the *cheapest*, most *savoury*, and most *nourishing* Food'.[4] This proved to be potato and barley soup, with croutons. Fed on this soup, Bavarian paupers would become healthy and energetic, or so Rumford insisted.

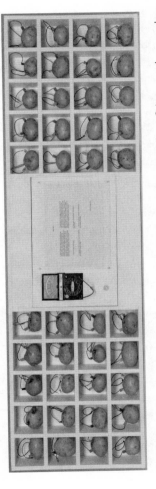

FIGURE 10 Victor Grippo, *Analogía I*, 1970–71. The Argentine artist Victor Grippo made a number of these assemblages, which he referred to as 'potatoes with cabling'. The small electrodes connecting the potatoes in *Analogía I* produce a measurable electrical current: a mass of potatoes generates energy. A mass of potato-eating labourers produces profit, or so argued political economists such as Adam Smith. Grippo's installations also reflect the collective power of individuals. Perhaps the energy provided by the lowly potato can be used to create a more just society. Grippo's artwork provokes us to consider how the collective power of ordinary people can be appropriated for the benefit of others, as well as how it can become a source of liberation. Harvard Art Museums/Fogg Museum, Richard Norton Memorial Fund and gift of Leslie Cheek, Jr., 2010.3, and Imaging Department, © President and Fellows of Harvard College.

Potatoes would render useful citizens from the gristle of the useless poor. The Argentine artist Víctor Grippo's *Analogía I* reflects rather precisely Rumford's vision of the potato's transformative power. In Grippo's installation rows of small, vulnerable potatoes have been pierced with electrical sensors, to provide energy for some larger purpose. The image may be taken to symbolize 'the people whose collective power is controlled by the authoritarian state'.[5] A great deal of potato translates into a more powerful state.

Rumford calculated the cost of preparing his soup in great detail, but he made clear that simple economy was not his sole focus. The food also needed to be tasty. Citing Hippocrates, he insisted that 'whatever pleases the palate nourishes'. This was why his soup demanded croutons. Croutons, he explained, required extended chewing, which 'prolongs the duration of the enjoyment of eating, a matter of very great importance indeed, and which has not hitherto been sufficiently attended to'. Seizing the moral high ground, Rumford insisted that most people dismissed the notion that the poor were entitled to happiness, but he did not. 'The enjoyments which fall to the lot of the bulk of mankind are not so numerous as to render an attempt to increase them superfluous', he observed piously.[6] His potato soup, with its chewy croutons, would cheer up even the most miserable of Munich's beggars. It's unlikely that Grippo's little potatoes will themselves benefit from the electrical matrix in which they are imprisoned, but Rumford was certain that Munich's poor would themselves gain enormously from his soup.

It's pretty clear that the croutons were a way of eking out a small amount of soup, and it's anyone's guess how much Munich's beggars truly enjoyed Rumford's concoction; the responses were mixed when I tried some out of a group of friends. But Rumford's insistence on pleasure was absolutely typical of soup enthusiasts. The hungry years of the 1790s, as war raged across Europe, saw the creation of Rumford-inspired soup kitchens in many European cities. Rumford himself set one up at the London Foundling Hospital in 1796; by 1800 there were nearly fifty such establishments in the British capital alone.[7] More were formed elsewhere in Germany, and in Switzerland, Italy, Sweden, Spain and France. All this soup was intended to pre-empt political activism and revolt inspired by the French Revolution, and to assuage the severe shortages prompted by harvest failures, warfare and ill-conceived state agricultural policies, but it promised happiness.

Neither the residents in the Munich poorhouse nor the inmates at the other charity kitchens doling out potato soup truly had much choice about what they ate; *personal choice* was nonetheless a central concept animating Rumford's interpretation of his scheme. According to Rumford, the beneficiaries of his soup had at first been unenthusiastic about the inclusion of potatoes, but once they tasted the result their scepticism vanished. 'The Poor', he reported, 'are now grown so fond of potatoes that they would not easily be satisfied without them.'[8] Poor people, he believed, were choosing potato soup, and this multitude of individual choices would together build a stronger and more powerful state. Public health was thus framed as a matter of individual choice.

Invisible hands

It is no coincidence that this faith in a wonderful confluence of individual dietary choice and public good emerged at exactly the moment as the tenets of classical economics were being developed. The best way to ensure flourishing commerce, its advocates insisted, was to let people look after their own well-being. Adam Smith expressed these new ideas clearly in his limpid prose: Smith's 1776 *An Inquiry into the Nature and Causes of the Wealth of Nations* proposed that if individuals were properly empowered to do this, the combination of a myriad self-interested actions would form a well-functioning economic system. In Smith's opinion,

> Every individual is continually exerting himself to find out the most advantageous employment for whatever capital he can command. It is his own advantage, indeed, and not that of the society, which he has in view. But the study of his own advantage naturally, or rather necessarily leads him to prefer that employment which is most advantageous to the society.[9]

The individual pursuit of personal advantage thus lay behind a successful economy, which would in turn deliver greater happiness to all. The worst thing the state could do was to try to intervene in the market. Interventions in the food market were seen as particularly pernicious, and likely to provoke the very shortages that they aimed to prevent. This rather novel idea began to be expressed in the early eighteenth century and became increasingly common as the Enlightenment progressed. As everyone knows, faith in the free market is now a cornerstone of modern capitalism. These ideas profoundly shape our world.

It was perhaps inevitable that Adam Smith should particularly recommend potatoes. His economic theorizations were premised on the conviction that national wealth was possible only when the population was happy. No society, he insisted, could be 'flourishing and happy, of which the far greater part of the members are poor and miserable'. Economic growth, he believed, provided the circumstances for the majority 'to be the happiest and the most comfortable'. Happiness and comfort, in turn, required a plentiful supply of pleasant and nutritious food, and this is what potatoes offered. Not only was the potato far more productive than wheat – Smith, like the FAO, calculated that land planted with potatoes would produce three times the quantity of nourishment as land laid to wheat – but it was also easier to cultivate, and, crucially, was an 'agreeable and wholesome variety of food'. He made a point of stressing that potatoes were eaten by 'the strongest men and the most beautiful women' in Britain, who turn out, rather surprisingly, to be Irish labourers and prostitutes. 'No food can afford a more decisive proof of its nourishing quality, or of its being peculiarly suitable to the health of the human constitution', he concluded.[10]

Smith linked the personal benefits individuals would derive from a greater consumption of potatoes to a greater flourishing of the economy. If planted with potatoes, agricultural land would support a larger population, who would produce a greater surplus. This would benefit workers, landlords and the overall economy. In Smith's happy vision, as in that of William Buchan and countless other potato advocates, if individuals chose to eat more potatoes, the benefits would accrue to everyone. Better input of potatoes would result in better economic outputs.

In keeping with the principles that underpinned Smith's model of political economy and agricultural improvement, he did not recommend that people be *obliged* to grow and eat potatoes. His emphasis rather was on the natural alignment of individual and national interest. Indeed, potential tensions between personal and public interest were addressed directly by a number of potato promoters, concerned precisely to see off any suggestion that they were subordinating individual agency to collective well-being. John Sinclair, president of the British Board of Agriculture in the 1790s and an enthusiastic potato advocate, observed that some people might imagine farmers should be left to make their own decisions about whether to grow potatoes or other recommended crops. This view, he insisted, was misguided. 'If the public were to *dictate* to the farmer how he was to cultivate his grounds', this might, he admitted, 'be the source of infinite mischief'. Providing information to inform individual choice, however, 'instead of being mischievous, must be attended with the happiest consequences'.[11]

It is precisely through this sort of idealized, and highly ideological, convergence that the supposedly free choices of individuals have come to form the theoretical foundations of the modern, liberal state. Our uneasy conviction that what we eat is entirely our own business, but what other people eat probably has an impact on us all, is born of this marriage between political economy and eighteenth-century statecraft.

Choosing potatoes

Advice and information, rather than legislation, remain the preferred techniques for transforming global and national food systems for many policymakers. Public health initiatives aimed at modifying eating practices consistently collide with the principles of individual choice that lie at the heart of liberalism. During the Second World War, deficiencies of the US diet were identified as a threat to national security after a shockingly large number of army recruits were rejected on the grounds of ill health attributed to bad diet. Government officials established a wide-ranging programme of dietary reform aimed not only at managing the United States' limited food resources but also at improving national health by changing the nation's eating habits. Eating a nutritionally balanced meal was cast as a patriotic duty, a necessary contribution to the war effort. Nonetheless, this wartime emphasis on changing individual diets unsettled the very body charged with implementing these transformations. The federal Committee on Food Habits suspected that such interventions were fundamentally incompatible with liberal democracy. It fretted that by trying to alter eating habits the government was encouraging the sort of submissive rule-following it believed characteristic of totalitarian regimes. Real Americans would, and should, resist such dietary guidance.[12]

What we eat matters to us; we're not certain whether it ought to matter to anyone else. We generally insist that our diets are entirely our concern, and resent being told to eat more fruit, drink less alcohol, and generally pull our socks up when it comes to dinner. The effort in 2012 by New York City mayor Michael Bloomberg to ban the sale of extra-large soft drinks failed because critics viewed it as an intrusion into the individual's right to make their own dietary mistakes. 'New Yorkers need a Mayor, not a Nanny', shouted a full-page advert in the *New York Times*. 'You only *thought* you lived in the land of the free', it warned. The advertisement was funded by the Center for Consumer Freedom, a lobbying group linked to the fast-food and tobacco industries. Its campaigns are framed around the concept of choice. Like the wartime Committee on Food Habits, it interprets interventions in personal eating habits as the thin edge of an illiberal wedge. Soda bans will lead ultimately to the loss of 'our basic freedoms'. According to the Center's founder,

> A growing cabal of activists has meddled in Americans' lives in recent years. They include self-anointed 'food police', health campaigners, trial lawyers, personal-finance do-gooders, animal-rights misanthropes, and meddling bureaucrats. Their common denominator? They all claim to know 'what's best for you'. In reality, they're eroding our basic freedoms – the freedom to buy what we want, eat what we want, drink what we want, and raise our children as we see fit.

It isn't only US lobby groups that view consumer food choice as a fundamental human right. When a school near Rotherham, in the north of England, eliminated deep-fried Turkey Twizzlers and fizzy drinks from its canteen, outraged mothers rose in protest, insisting that their children had the right to eat potato crisps, burgers and other unhealthy food. We can trace the hostility to Bloomberg's soda ban, and the unrest in Rotherham, back to the Enlightenment.[13]

The scene portrayed in Vincent van Gogh's *Potato Eaters* encapsulates the sort of impoverished choice landscape opposed by the Center for Consumer Freedom. The painting depicts a peasant family sitting at supper. Van Gogh was pleased with the painting, for he believed he had captured something essential about peasant life. Perhaps, he suggested optimistically, he had managed to produce 'a REAL PEASANT PAINTING' – the block capitals signalling his excitement at this achievement.[14] He intended the painting to help 'civilized people' like himself understand the beauty and authenticity of peasant life. 'You see', he wrote to his brother,

> I really have wanted to make it so that people get the idea that these folk, who are eating their potatoes by the light of their little lamp, have tilled the earth themselves with these hands they are putting in the dish, and so it speaks of MANUAL LABOUR and – that they have thus honestly *earned* their food. I wanted it to give the idea of a wholly different way of life from ours – civilized people.

His painting, he wrote, smelled of bacon, potato steam and smoke. It showed the peasantry as it truly was, as 'not being able to be other than one is'.

The Potato Eaters is a beautiful painting. Van Gogh likened its muted colour scheme to the subtle effects achieved by Scottish tartan, with its overlapping light and dark threads. At the same time, it unsettles us. John Coveney, an expert on public health and always instructive on food and the ethics of eating, observes that we can explain this reaction in part through the language of choice. 'Because choice and the freedom to choose have become part of the normative category of food', he writes, 'not having choice is regarded as a situation in need of correction'.[15] This peasant family, as Van Gogh put it, cannot be other than it is. They have no option

FIGURE 11 Vincent van Gogh, *The Potato Eaters*, 1885. Van Gogh was proud that in this picture he had captured the reality of peasant life. The simple meal of potatoes enjoyed by his subjects has been earned through honest, manual labour. 'I so often think that the peasants are a world in themselves, so much better in many respects than the civilized world', he wrote to his brother Theo. Viewers, in contrast, have generally viewed the dinner of potatoes as a sign of deprivation, not a source of dignity. Today, a lack of choice is often seen as 'a situation in need of correction'. Van Gogh Museum, Amsterdam (Vincent van Gogh Foundation).

but to eat potatoes. It is this, as much as anything else, that makes them an instructive object lesson for 'civilized people' such as Van Gogh, or us.

Probably we civilized people don't want to live in the world of Van Gogh's potato eaters. Where do we want to live? In the New York City of 32-ounce soft drinks? In Rotherham primary schools during the brief period when foods consisting of deep-fried turkey, pork fat and hydrogenated vegetable oil were banned from cafeterias? Where?

Responsibilization

'As I took my fifth potato, she leaned across, with clasped hands and tearful eyes, and breathed imploringly, "Oh, Mr Thackeray! Don't!"'.[16]

Should we eat more potatoes? Potato consumption is rising rapidly in Asia and the developing world more generally, at the same time that it is falling in the West. Scientific assessment of the potato's healthfulness is divided. It is low in fat, rich in vitamins and minerals, and may hold other beneficial medical properties. Recent investigations suggest that purple-fleshed varieties contain compounds that impede the spread of prostate cancer, and the potato's antioxidants may also protect against stomach cancer and cardiovascular disease. Other studies convey less cheery findings. A report published in the *British Medical Journal* in 2016 linked higher intakes of most forms of potato with an increased risk of hypertension. Baked, boiled, mashed, fried: all were equally pernicious.[17] They've long been considered fattening. While this was a positive quality to eighteenth-century physicians such as William Buchan, by the mid-nineteenth century slimness, rather than plumpness, had become the modern goal. The potato's status fell accordingly. 'To the scientist there is nothing so tragic on earth as the sight of a fat man eating a potato', declared the slimming guru Vance Thompson in his 1914 classic *Eat and Grow Thin*. Presumably something along these lines explains why Charlotte Brönte was so dismayed when her idol William Makepeace Thackeray, author of *Vanity Fair* and a little on the stout side, ate a fifth potato when she invited him to dinner in 1850.[18]

The pleasure we experience in eating was not always considered a threat to our health. For millennia it was an accepted fact that your body was best able to digest, and therefore gain nourishment from, foods you enjoyed, like, perhaps, potatoes. This appealing notion was medical orthodoxy until scientific investigations in the nineteenth century cast cold water on it. The more nineteenth-century scientists learned about the digestive process the less importance they ascribed to pleasure: a healthy diet was one that provided optimal nutrition, but that had nothing to do with how a food tasted. In fact, a diet guided by pleasure was probably inimical to good health, as it was likely to seduce the eater into the consumption of unhealthy and nutritionally empty foods. 'Pleasure', writes this historian Charlotte Biltekoff, 'was viewed as a threat to the reign of scientific reason in the kitchen, tempting eaters towards both caloric and economic forms of excess'. Ellen Richards, the nineteenth-century founder of 'home economics' as a discipline, insisted that 'in food, not what *we like* but what is good for the many should be the standard'.[19]

As Richards's comment reminds us, what we eat has an impact on everyone else. If everyone surrenders to the fleeting pleasure of deep-fried potato crisps and sugary drinks, then, in a dreadful reversal of the Enlightenment's virtuous 'potatoes-are-good-for-us-and-good-for-the-body-politic' cycle, we, and the body politic, will be beset by obesity, diabetes and other ills. Economists calculate the economic costs of our collective failure to eat properly; one survey placed the figure at well over fifty billion dollars for the United States alone.[20] Perhaps pleasure, and choice, are sirens, seducing us into the rocks.

Or perhaps the problem is that we have misguided ideas about what we like. Perhaps we need to retrain our taste buds so that we actually enjoy the things that are good for the many, and for ourselves. The alternative food movement shows great confidence in the corrective power of listening closely to our senses, which will ultimately lead the eater towards the right foods. Eating a locally grown, low intensity, unprocessed diet is, in the words of the food writer Michael Pollan, 'conducive not only to better health but also to greater pleasure in eating, two goals that turn out to be mutually reinforcing'.[21] I think that's true, but then I would, since as many critics have observed, middle-class women like myself are eager consumers of this approach to food and the ethics of eating.

The historian Charlotte Biltekoff believes that our current celebration of the gustatory pleasures of healthy foods in fact fits perfectly into a neoliberal model of the individual. It is the individual who is responsible for cultivating the discrimination necessary to enjoy the right foods, and for developing the self-control to avoid the wrong ones. Healthy eating is framed as an opportunity for personal responsibility and choice. 'One of the things I talk a lot about is the need to really work on cultural change in America to encourage a culture of personal responsibility', stated George W. Bush in a lecture about the HealthierUS initiative, launched in 2002 to promote 'healthier lifestyles' through diet and exercise schemes. HealthierUS, Bush continued, 'really appeals to personal responsibility, doesn't it? It says that we are responsible to our own health'.[22]

Bush's comments reflect the process of 'responsibilization', making individuals, rather than, say, the national government or larger socio-economic structures, responsible for things like their own health. Responsibilization encourages us to evaluate our own success in eating properly, and links success to positive character traits such as self-control. If like Thackeray we're overweight because we've eaten too many potatoes, then it's our own fault, as well as a tragic sight. 'Negative attitudes towards the obese are highly correlated with negative attitudes towards minorities and the poor, such as the belief that all these groups are lazy and lack self-control and will power', notes a 2006 study.[23]

Such hapless eaters perfectly embody the surplus people identified by the philosophers Michel Foucault and Giorgio Agamben as obstacles to the modern state. In a number of his works Foucault contrasted the modern state's approach to managing the population with earlier forms of political power. For the modern state, he believed, power is not a matter of executing criminals and not executing everyone else. Rather it is about fostering the well-being of some sections of the population and removing all support from those whose well-being it does not wish to promote. 'One might say', he observed, that in modern times 'the ancient right to *take* life or *let* live was replaced by a power to *foster* life or *disallow* it to the point of death'.[24]

The population, the productive members of society, should be nurtured, helped to live and flourish. It is precisely such ideas that contributed to the rise, in the eighteenth century, of the conviction that the strength and security of the state depended on the vigour and productivity of the population. As Foucault described it, this new relationship between individuals and the state comprised

> a circle that starts from the state as a power of rational and calculated intervention on individuals and comes back to the state as a growing set of forces, or forces to be developed, passing through the life of individuals, which will now be precious to the state simply as life. ... This circle, with all that this implies, ... must succeed in linking together the state's strength and individual felicity. This felicity, as the individual's better than just living, must in some way be drawn on and constituted into state utility: making men's happiness the state's utility, making men's happiness the very strength of the state.[25]

This, he argued, was the first time in the history of Western societies that 'the being and well-being of individuals really became relevant for government intervention'. This is why its eighteenth-century promoters so often insisted that the potato offered a high road to personal happiness.

From within the logic of this modern form of statecraft, however, there are others who are not part of the population. They are just people, and they are in the way, like the tobacco-smoking, potato-eating Irishmen who annoyed William Petty, or their equally unproductive descendants in the 1840s, abandoned by Trevelyan to their necessary fate. The modern state sees no compelling reason to encourage their existence. Modern politics, Foucault argued, is a matter of both 'making live' and 'letting die'. The Italian philosopher Giorgio Agamben has written a great deal about the dismal fate of those whom the state 'lets die' – the marginal, the stateless, those whose lives are deemed 'unworthy of being lived' and from whom support is withdrawn. In his view, we all teeter on the edge of this abyss, potential outsiders constantly at risk of being left to die.[26]

What to do, then, about all these troublesome people, with their fast food and cigarettes, disrupting the system and falling ill? In our health-valuing culture, writes the cultural critic Robert Crawford, 'people come to define themselves in part by how well they succeed or fail in adopting healthy practices and by the qualities of character or personality believed to support healthy behaviours. They assess others by the same criteria'.[27] Away with the Unhealthy Other, this impediment to our happiness and the strength of the state! At the same time, Crawford writes, even the most assiduous attention to personal health 'cannot deliver the symbolic assurances needed to offset either anxieties about the dangers of a toxic society *or* the deepening insecurities of contemporary … life'. And how many of us truly conform to the dictates of healthy living? We are hardly the masters of our own destiny when it comes to diet. What analysts call our 'obesogenic' environment seems likely to outweigh any attempt at nudging us towards better eating habits, and when given the opportunity to choose, few of us routinely make wise decisions either with our wallets or our meals. We can't quite decide what to do with these problem eaters weighing down the body politic, in part because we suspect they might be us.

5 POTATO PHILOSOPHY

Giving thanks for potatoes

The Angelus by Jean-François Millet shows two peasants offering thanks for their meagre harvest of potatoes. Millet's original title for the painting was *Prayer for the Potato Crop*. Millet painted many sympathetic scenes of rural life in northern France, including a number of other depictions of potato cultivation; his work conveys both the beauty of the landscape around the village of Barbizon and the difficult, exhausting existence of agricultural labourers. *The Angelus* reflects what the philosopher Raymond Boisvert called 'stomach time': the sensation of hunger, which obeys neither the smooth flowing continuum, nor objective externality, of clock time.[1] Millet's peasants are hungry, and they will probably remain hungry after they have eaten their potatoes. Potatoes cannot guarantee to keep away hunger, no matter what eighteenth-century potato enthusiasts promised. At the same time, Millet's hungry peasants are praying, not protesting. Many nineteenth-century viewers praised the 'naive faith' and reassuring acceptance of inequality that they detected in the painting's protagonists. Others criticized the work as conservative for endorsing poverty (and potatoes).[2]

The ideological implications of the eighteenth-century celebration of the potato as a wonder food did not pass unnoticed. The very encouragement to eat potatoes endowed

FIGURE 12 Jean-François Millet, *The Angelus*, 1857–59. Contemplating their small basket of potatoes, Millet's peasants display the gratitude potato promoters encouraged. Viewers in late-nineteenth-century France admired the docile faith they detected in the couple's evening prayer. It seems unlikely that this pair will emulate the recalcitrant behaviour of the agricultural workers who rioted in 1830s England under the banner 'We will not live upon potatoes'. Jean-François Millet: *L'Angélus*, 1857–59 (RF 1877), Paris, Musée d'Orsay, from the estate of Alfred Chauchard, 1910.

the tuber with a powerful symbolic resonance. For those suspicious of the new models of statecraft, the capitalist potato represented nothing less than a tool of exploitation. 'We will not live upon potatoes', read a banner unfurled in the English county of Kent during the 1830 'Captain Swing' riots. The upheaval, which mobilized thousands of rural workers across England, was essentially a protest against the transformation of English agriculture into a fully capitalist system. By the 1820s, many rural labourers, as the historians Eric Hobsbawm and George Rudé put it, had become 'not merely a full proletarian, but an underemployed, pauperised one'. During the Swing riots, large groups of agricultural workers confronted farmers to insist on higher wages and the improvement of working conditions. When requests were not sufficient they sometimes set fire to barns and destroyed agricultural machinery such as the threshing machines that reduced the demand for their labour.[3]

For protestors, 'potatoes' were part of the exploitative system they rejected. In the Sussex village of Pulborough, a group of between thirty and forty labourers gathered in the vestry room of the church to explain to the farmers who had come to listen that they had been 'starving on potatoes long enough, and there must be an alternation'. The banner brandished in Kent expressed the same sentiment. Their objection wasn't to the potato as such. These men and women undoubtedly ate potatoes regularly; their quarrel was with the potato as an ideology. 'Living on potatoes' offered a shorthand for the entire system that the protestors rejected.[4]

Such sceptics recognized that the potato had been enlisted as a foot soldier in the campaign of capitalism. They also recognized that encouragement to eat potatoes often emanated, as one sardonic observer commented in 1800, from 'philosophers, who, to their immortal honour, studied *substitutes for bread* upon a *full belly*'.[5] Potatoes were a 'food for others', to recall the title of Subodh Gupta's inedible metallic potatoes. Such recommendations were epitomized in the complaisant observation of the warden of Merton College, Oxford, during the hard winter of 1842 to 1843, that if workers could not afford to buy bread, at least they 'rejoiced in potatoes'.[6] In refusing to give thanks for potatoes, Captain Swing rioters rejected something much larger than the potato itself: the conversion of the English economy into a fully capitalist system.

The potato can't be separated from this larger history. The larger history is part of what a potato means, what a potato *is*. Anthropologists warn us against trying too hard to distinguish between concrete things and the meanings they create. If we aim simply to put things (like potatoes) in their larger social, cultural and political contexts, in order to get at their symbolic meaning, then in the end we don't really need to study the things themselves at all. Artefacts, objects, things, become mere illustrations of some larger framework, 'exemplars or reflections of meanings which are produced elsewhere'.[7] If, however, we try to consider the objects and their meanings as one and the same, as mutually constitutive, then we can think in new ways not only about the objects, but also about the frameworks. This, I suggest, is the case with potatoes. Potatoes are part of how we understand famine, or survival, or the experience of being governed. They are not simply illustrations some larger process.

The anthropologist Nancy Ries shows this neatly in her discussion of the many meanings of 'potato' in post-Soviet Russia. The economic collapse of the 1990s cut deep. The real value of cash incomes halved between 1990 and 2000 and Russia's entire socio-economic structure underwent a brusque reorientation. Potatoes became a way of articulating the experience of crisis. When asked how they got by, people answered 'potato': '*kartofel*' or its diminutive '*kartoshka*'. 'We survive on potato.' 'Russia lives on potato.' 'If not for our potato plots, I do not know how we would survive'. Such statements are far more than a simple description of household ecology. In fact, it's not at all clear that potatoes truly played a pivotal role in ensuring domestic food security during this period. Rather, 'potato' was a way to narrate the experience of marginalization from the new forms of political and social organization under construction in post-Soviet Russia. It is also a way to insist on the possibility of survival in the face of enormous odds. In doing this, it transforms the messiness of lived experience into something new, into a narrative. Potatoes, Ries writes, sit 'on the cusp between desperate hope and the terror of insecurity; the same moment, in the same breath, potato shouts both "we can survive" and "God help us now"'. Potatoes tell a story. They make a history, which is to say, they create meaning out of experience.[8]

Taking a page from work by the philosophers Andy Clark and David Chalmers, we might also consider the potato an extension of our own mind, an external hard drive where we store ideas and thoughts. Clark and Chalmers argued that the boundary between our minds and the rest of the world isn't terribly sharp; there's no red line on the map showing where thinking stops, and the outside world begins. We use all sorts of 'extensions', from books to smart phones, to help us think. These extensions form part of our overall store of what Clark and Chalmers called cognitive resources.[9]

So perhaps a potato can be a cognitive resource to help us make sense of our place in the world. Perhaps they are part of how we think, about hunger, about survival, and about our relationship with each other.

Family histories (written with my sister Susan)

'Do you want any of these?' Our mother is clearing the house in anticipation of a move. Little by little a vast collection of stuff is being winnowed to the things that really matter. Our ingenious mother is rightly proud of the new homes she's found for objects that haven't made it onto the final list, from our father's vast collection of vinyl records to her mother-in-law's monstrous punch bowl with its brood of cut-glass cups. My sister, custodian of family history, takes mountains of documents, from schoolwork to marriage certificates to obituaries.

But what to do with all the recipes? All the pages scissored out of magazines, the 3x5 index cards carefully sorted into plastic boxes, the handwritten sheets of paper. I study some, conscious that they are a memory bank. I find a page written by our Austrian grandfather, explaining how to prepare potato noodles.

Georg Deutsch's recipe for Potato Noodles: '6 boiled, pared potatoes, 1 egg, ½ t salt, 1 c sifted flour, 1 c fine breadcrumbs, 2 T butter, ¼ c confect. sugar. Press potatoes through strainer while warm. Blend with egg, salt. Stir in flour, adding more if needed to make workable dough. Knead well, make into sausage-like rolls. Cut into ½-inch pieces, roll into noodles, cook 10' in salted water. Meanwhile brown crumbs in butter. Drain noodles, coat them with crumb mixture, dust with sugar.'

Georg Deutsch travelled with our grandmother, our uncle Tom, and our infant mother from Vienna to Cleveland between 1938 and 1939. The rise of the Nazis made this expedient. We grew up with stories of 'the emigration', told by our grandmother, who recounted the challenges of cooking family meals on an illegal electric ring in a Paris hotel, but not the fact that she left her own mother behind on the platform in Vienna's Südbahnhof. In Cleveland, while Grandfather Georg went through the lengthy procedures to convert his Austrian medical qualifications into certificates that would allow him to practice in the United States – he had already Americanized his name to George – he and our grandmother tried their hand at strudel making, in the hope that it might provide a little income. The strudels led nowhere, but our memories of their Shaker Heights flat are infused with the tastes and aromas of their unfamiliar, delicious foods.

I try the potato noodles. This recipe is in English, written in our grandfather's distinctive hand. The measurements are in cups, not the metric grams that appear in some of his other recipes, the ones in German. A little story of assimilation on a scrap of paper. The noodles turn out to be flat gnocchi, served with buttered breadcrumbs. They're somewhat chewy, firm between the teeth.

Another box holds a neatly written card with a recipe for 'Anne Earle's potato rolls'.

Anne Earle's recipe for Potato Rolls: '1½ cups water, 1 package yeast or 3 tb of yeast, 1 c. mashed potatoes, ½ c. sugar, 2/3 c. shortening, 2 eggs – beaten, 7 to 7½ cups flour. Dissolve yeast in water. Mash potatoes, while hot add shortening, sugar & salt. Cool. Add 1 to 2 cups flour, stir in, add yeast, beaten eggs. Stir in remaining flour. Knead until smooth and elastic – 8 to 10 minutes. Grease bowl, cover with plastic bag. Refrigerate over night. Shape into rolls, let rise 1½ to 2 hrs. Bake 15. 400°.'

Anne Earle, our paternal grandmother, owner of the punch bowl, was born in 1901 on a dairy farm in Wisconsin. Her grandparents had emigrated from Wales in the 1840s, so we called her Nain, the Welsh for grandmother. Like most farms at the time, our grandmother's lacked running water and electric lights. Plumbing was installed in 1917, the same year that the family bought a Studebaker. Before that, on weekdays she twice a day walked the two miles from the farm to the one-room schoolhouse where she studied alongside some twenty other children of all ages. On Sundays the entire family traipsed back and forth to the church three times. The hours spent in church weren't for nothing; our Nain was Presbyterian to the core, and a teetotaller. (To her lasting disappointment, her descendants shared neither conviction, although we all tried to put up a good front.)

After graduating from Ripon College – where she roomed with a cousin who was briefly engaged to the actor Spencer Tracy – she taught mathematics at the American Indian Institute, in Wichita, Kansas. The Institute opened in 1920 with the aim of training up young Indian men as religious leaders. Its director was Henry Roe Cloud, the first Native American to attend Yale and himself an ordained Presbyterian. Church publications extolled the Institute's success in promoting 'racial uplift', and in helping its students play an active role as Christian citizens, while also retaining their indigenous identity. I'm certain the Institute must have grown potatoes during the years our grandmother was there, but I can't establish this.[10]

FIGURES 13 and 14 Anne and Clifford Earle, and her recipe for potato rolls. My grandmother Anne Earle was an excellent cook in the American vein. Her recipe for potato rolls, neatly copied onto a printed index card, is as much a piece of autobiography as is the eleven-page memoir she typed out in the same years. Women have left fewer written traces of their lives compared with men, but recipes can provide a rich source for women's history. Author's collection.

In 1930 Anne Griffith, as she then was, married Clifford Earle, like her a committed Presbyterian. Soon after marrying they moved to Chicago, where her husband attended McCormick Seminary and she worked as a secretary, at a salary of 25 cents an hour. Clifford's calling as a minister took them first to Racine, Wisconsin, where our father was born, and then back to Chicago and the neighbouring village of Oak Park. In 1947 our grandfather accepted a position on the Board of Christian Education at the Presbyterian Church and the family of three moved to the Philadelphia suburb of Abington.

Eating was a principal pleasure of childhood visits to their post-war bungalow. The sticky enjoyments of root beer and potato chips in their living room constitute some of Susan's strongest childhood memories, alongside her happy recollections of rosehip tea and pastries in Cleveland. On my birthday Nain sometimes made a hickory nut layer cake, iced with a molasses-sweet, praline frosting, the like of which I've never had since. She often baked fresh bread, served alongside strange, architectural constructions of lime Jell-O and Cool Whip, dishes of pickled watermelon rind, platters with soft, pink slices of utterly boneless, sinew-less roast beef and other foods that, even as children, we could tell did not come from the same universe that contained the challah and sour cherry jam we ate for breakfast in Cleveland. These treats originated in separate worlds that overlapped, or collided, with our own.

Nain's yeasted potato rolls are fluffy, sweet with egg and sugar, too light to fill you up, insubstantial but appealing.

They are no good for sandwiches, complains my English partner, but I like them. They remind me of our grandmother, of her dogged efforts to be of service to others, even when the tools at her disposal – a Jell-O salad, a belief in God – proved ineffective. Her potato rolls are as different from our grandfather's potato noodles as her life was from his.

Recipes tell family stories. 'Some women leave diaries. My mother left recipes', wrote Linda Murray Berzok.[11] Our grandmother Anne Earle did not leave a diary, although she did write an account of her childhood. Around 1985 she typed out an eleven-page family history, listing great-great grandparents, birth and death dates, and only the merest indication of her own thoughts or sentiments. She mentions 'difficult years' early in her marriage when money was scarce but she does not elaborate. Nor does she record what she felt, as she recovered in hospital from a hysterectomy, to learn that her mother had died, only a few months after her father had passed away. Neither does she express her feelings on leaving family, friends and her established position as a minister's wife in Oak Park for a new life in Abington, where there was no ready-made role for her. Although her relocation was smaller in scale than that of our other grandparents, who travelled from Vienna to Cleveland, she too had to construct a new life for herself. It was only late in his life that our father, in telling us about the challenges this move had posed to his own childhood, mused that it must have been hard for her as well. It was nothing he and his mother ever discussed.

It is in her recipes that one glimpses the close web of family that evidently sustained her. The tidy index cards list the origins of valued recipes. Some are entirely handwritten, as is the one for date cake. In the upper right-hand corner she has jotted 'Bobby', to show the recipe came from her niece Bobby Griffith. Other cards are pre-printed with spaces for the cook to write in the details: 'Recipe from the kitchen of: _____'. The card with the recipe for hickory nut cake reads 'Recipe from the kitchen of: Mother'. It lists only the ingredients; no instructions were needed to explain a procedure she witnessed first-hand. None of the other recipe are attributed to her mother and the recipe for nut cake is the only one to lack instructions. Recipes for cakes, pie and overly sugared breads far outnumber those for the pot roasts and casseroles that must have formed the backbone of her daily labour in the kitchen. A little something sweet in a life of deliberate sacrifice.

Our Austrian grandfather also composed a set of memoirs that recounted his memories of life in pre-war Austria, alongside other family histories, written as he lay dying of prostate cancer. Unlike Nain's matter-of-fact account, our grandfather's writings dive deeply into his feelings, and his persistent self-doubt. Despite working all his life as a GP, first in Vienna and then in Cleveland, he believed that he was not suited to the profession, a very painful realization. His marriage was terribly unhappy. 'Get me out of here' he begged our uncle from his sickbed in the Cleveland flat he shared with our grandmother. And Cleveland was no

Vienna. The upheaval of emigration and the scattering of his once-large family across four continents left him with few moorings. 'The dispersion of friends and relatives over the globe is terrifying – but apparently necessary', he wrote. He believed his far-flung web of connections worked against 'a narrow parochial spirit'. Migration in any event saved his life; neither my sister and I, nor our mother, would exist had our grandparents stayed in Vienna, which, apparently, was what

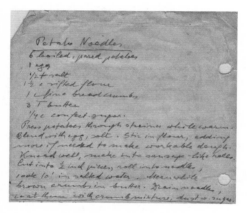

FIGURE 15 Georg Deutsch's recipe for potato noodles. Preparing my grandfather's handwritten recipe for potato noodles momentarily brought him back to life in my English kitchen. As I riced the potatoes and rolled the springy dough I imagined his hands performing the same actions, decades earlier, in the first-floor Cleveland flat where he lived with my grandmother. Remembering, as Toni Morrison argued, is a creative act. Author's collection.

would have happened had our grandmother not insisted they flee.

But resisting narrow parochialism comes at a price. 'Where am I at home?', he asked himself.

> Vienna? America? Honestly I don't know. I don't believe people of my sort feel truly at home anywhere. Like the dispersion of the family, this is terrifying and discomforting, but probably necessary.

I made a different sort of migration when I travelled to England in the 1980s as a scholarship student. I didn't intend to stay, but thirty years later I've not moved far from the house where I first leased a room. No one drove me from my birthplace; unlike our grandparents I wasn't obliged to sign a document promising never again to pollute the nation's soil with my unwelcome presence, and I can criss-cross the Atlantic as often as my budget (and attitude towards airplanes) permits. Even so our grandfather's words resonate with me. Wherever one journeys, the past trails along behind like a string of tin cans on a rope, banging and clattering, and reminding others that you're not from here. Potatoes have done a better job of blending into new environments than our grandfather and I have.

Our grandparents' memoirs tell part of their stories, but so too do the potato rolls, the potato noodles. Making their recipes is a form of conjuring, of summoning them up, of remembering them. Like Toni Morrison's concept of re-memory, making such recipes is an active process of remembrance that takes place not only in my head but also in the warm mound of riced potatoes on a wooden board, in the soft belly of risen dough nestling in a glass bowl. Classicists employ the term ekphrasis to describe creative practices that bring to life the nature or essence of a work of art from a different genre. A poem describing a painting, or a piece of music inspired by a novel are examples of ekphrasis. I think that preparing our grandparents' recipes is an ekphrastic act, an evocation of their lives through the art of cooking. Cooking, perhaps humanity's oldest form of art, momentarily condenses the entire history that led to these two recipes into a single potato roll, a single dish of potato noodles sprinkled with buttered bread crumbs.

The consolation of potatoes

While awaiting execution the sixth-century Roman philosopher Boethius composed a meditation on the human condition called *The Consolation of Philosophy*. Boethius had lately suffered a tremendous reversal of fortunes. At the time of his arrest he was a high-ranking official in the service of the emperor Theodoric, king of the Ostrogoths. Disagreements between Boethius and his erstwhile patron resulted first in the philosopher's imprisonment, and then his death. *The Consolation of Philosophy* was both a response to these events, and a larger exploration on the aims and ends of life. It consists of a dialogue between Boethius and Lady Philosophy, who together discuss the nature of happiness, the origins of evil, and the transcendence of divine love. It was, for the next thousand years, enormously influential and widely read. Scholars are divided over whether Lady Philosophy succeeded in offering Boethius the inner peace he sought, but the book makes clear that insofar as earthly happiness was possible, it lay not in worldly fame but in self-knowledge, in philosophy.

The consolation of potatoes is more modest, but also philosophical. It lies in their solid ordinariness, in their ability to root us into the common ground. The Estonian composer Arvo Pärt commented in 2016 that when overwhelmed by the challenge of composition he sought refuge in potatoes. On such occasions, he told *Gramophone* magazine, 'I peel potatoes, that calms me down'. This routine, domestic task through its very concreteness facilitates the creative work of the imagination. The contemplative act of peeling a potato refocuses the mind away from the outer world, into an inner space of creativity and solace. Seamus Heaney perhaps experienced something similar as he sat peeling potatoes with his mother, the silence broken by little pleasant splashes of peel falling into a basin of water, a memory he described in one of his most beloved poems.[12]

Pierre Bezukhov, the protagonist of Tolstoy's *War and Peace*, also found comfort in a potato. Tolstoy's novel, set during Napoleon's unsuccessful invasion of Russia in the early nineteenth century, is ultimately concerned with the place of the individual in the impersonal sweep of history. For Tolstoy, the value of human life lay precisely in its prosaic ordinariness, in the small virtues that bind us together. Over the course of the novel Pierre journeys from a state of isolation and despair towards an appreciation that he forms part of a web of connections linking not simply men and women, but the entire universe. This new appreciation develops through an encounter with a man and a baked potato.

Pierre has been captured by French troops, together with innumerable other Russians. Disoriented and desolate, Pierre languishes in a dark hut, isolated from himself and others. At length he perceives another presence, in whom he senses 'something pleasant, soothing and rounded'. His fellow prisoner is a peasant, Platon Karataev, who offers Pierre a baked potato with salt, together with advice that represents Tolstoy's own world view. The simple potato sprinkled with salt encapsulates the message that Karataev conveys: get on with others and be grateful for what you have. The earthy potato provides a still centre point in the maelstrom of history that spins around Pierre, symbolizing both the consolation of small things, and also humanity itself. Munching his potato, Pierre muses that he has never tasted anything better in his life. Karataev's solid, salty potato helps restore in the despairing Pierre some sense of hope. A consolation indeed.

The sturdy, round Karataev and his baked potato mirror each other, and in their solidity and concreteness help Pierre appreciate his own connections to the cosmos. Looking up at the starry sky, Pierre comes to realize that 'All that is mine, all that is in me, all that is me!'. The straightforward prayer that Karataev offers at bedtime reiterates the message of the potato: 'Lord, lay me down like a stone, raise me up like a loaf'.[13] Bread, a stone, a potato, each person, life itself, flow into each other. From the stony potato life rises up.

ACKNOWLEDGEMENTS

So many people have talked with me about potatoes, about watching their father repair a potato spinner, or about the burning sensation that to this day spreads across their palm when they see a boiled potato, a consequence of their grandmother's dictum, sixty years earlier, that the best way to peel a hot potato is to hold it in your hand. Without these stories I'd never have written *Potato*. They taught me that when you say 'potato' the response is often an autobiography. Potatoes provide a way for us to speak about ourselves. I'm deeply grateful for the generosity with which acquaintances have shared their memories.

I'm also indebted to the many colleagues who have collaborated with the potato project by sending me references, suggesting lines of inquiry, and listening to me drone on. Some particularly stalwart souls read drafts of the manuscript and did their best to correct my mistakes. Others guided me through philosophical thickets, helped me understand contemporary China, and translated material that would otherwise have remained impenetrable. I don't really know where to begin when it comes to thanking them. The most telegraphic list should include Pia Campeggiani, Roger Cooter, Helen Curry, Anne Gerritsen, Anandi Hattiangadi, Gretchen Henderson, John King, Jakob Klein, Claudia Stein and Keith Tribe, and really many others as well.

Potato was born in the tranquil grounds of the Swedish Collegium for Advanced Studies, in Uppsala. The generosity of the European Institutes for Advanced Studies fellowship programme, as well as the Collegium's visionary approach to collegiality, enabled me to convert a conviction that potatoes were important into this account. I'm also grateful to the John Carter Brown Library for welcoming me into their supportive and stimulating community of researchers.

Lastly, I thank my family for their amused patience and support. Matt Western ('as in the film') didn't merely tolerate my extended absences; he indulged and sustained me throughout this project. My mother Lisa Earle shared her deep expertise in plant breeding, put me in touch with colleagues, and kept me up-to-date with scientific developments. One could not hope for a better companion, or mother. My beloved father died shortly before I began writing this book; I have been fortunate to have a father who provided such unstinting love, the most powerful legacy a parent can bequeath. Most of all, I would like to thank my sister Susan. Her gift for telling stories reflects her sensitivity to our emotional innerscapes, as well as an ear for language that Ogden Nash would envy. And what a cook! *Potato* is dedicated to her, and to the memory of Clifford Earle.

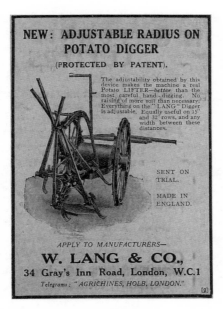

FIGURE 16 Mechanised Potato Digger, 1919. Potato diggers, like the digging sticks wielded by Guamon Poma's Andean potato-harvesters, allow potatoes to be grown on slopes too steep for conventional mechanised machinery to negotiate. They were used in the Channel Islands up until the 1950s to harvest Jersey royals and other new potatoes. Advertisement from W. Lang and Co of 34 Gray's Inn Road, London, Grace's Guide to British Industrial History, https://www.gracesguide.co.uk/W._Lang_and_Co.

LIST OF FIGURES

NOTES

Introduction

1 Kevin Lui, 'Is This the World's Most Photogenic Potato? Photo Sells for $1.08m', *CNN*, 27 January 2016, http://edition.cnn.com/style/article/potato-photo-million-euros/index.html (accessed 13 April 2018).

2 Karl Marx, 'The Eighteenth Brumaire of Louis Napoleon', *Marx's Eighteenth Brumaire: (Post)modern Interpretations*, eds Mark Cowling and James Martin, trans. Terrell Carver (London: Pluto Press, 2002, [1852]), 101.

3 FAOSTAT, Food and Agriculture Organization of the United Nations, http://www.fao.org/faostat/en/#data (accessed 13 April 2018).

4 Gaspar Mollien, *Travels in the Republic of Colombia in the Years 1822 and 1823* (London, 1824), 198; and Subodh Gupta, personal communication, 13 January 2017.

5 O. Soffer, J.M. Adovasio and D.C. Hyland, 'The 'Venus' Figures: Textiles, Basketry, Gender, and Status in the Upper Paleolithic', *Current Anthropology* 41:4 (2000): 511–37; and April Nowell and Melanie Chang, 'Science, the Media, and Interpretations of Upper Paleolithic Figures', *American Anthropologist* 116:3 (2014): 562–77.

Chapter 1

1   Jan Douwe van der Ploeg, 'Potatoes and Knowledge', in *An Anthropological Critique of Development: The Growth of Ignorance*, ed. Mark Hobart (London: Routledge, 1993), 221.

2   Donald Ugent, Tom Dillehay and Carlos Ramírez, 'Potato Remains from a Late Pleistocene Settlement in Southcentral Chile', *Economic Botany* 41:1 (1987): 17–27; and Lisbeth Louderback and Bruce Pavlik, 'Starch Granule Evidence for the Earliest Potato Use in North America', *Proceedings of the National Academy of Sciences* 114:29 (18 July 2017): 7606–10.

3   Pedro de Cieza de León, *Parte primera de la Chronica del Peru* (Antwerp, 1554), 274–6.

4   Felipe Guaman Poma de Ayala, *El primer nueva corónica y buen gobierno*, 1615–16, The Guaman Poma Website, Det Kongelige Bibliotek, Copenhagen, www.kb.dk/permalink/2006/poma/info/en/frontpage.htm (accessed 13 April 2018).

5   John Murra, 'Rite and Crop in the Inca State', in *Culture in History: Essays in Honor of Paul Radin*, ed. Stanley Diamond (New York: Octagon, 1960), 393–407.

6   Irene Silverblatt, *Moon, Sun, and Witches: Gender Ideologies and Class in Inca and Colonial Peru* (Princeton: Princeton University Press, 1987), 27.

7   Van der Ploeg, 'Potatoes and Knowledge', 221.

8   Elizabeth Benson, 'Moche Art: Myth, History and Rite', in *The Spirit of Ancient Peru: Treasures from the Museo Arqueológico Rafael Larco Herrera*, ed. Kathleen Berrin (London: Thames and Hudson, 1997), 45.

9   Seamus Heaney, 'At a Potato Digging', *Death of a Naturalist* (London: Faber and Faber, 1991 [1966]), 20.

10 L.A. Clarkson and E. Margaret Crawford, *Feast and Famine: Food and Nutrition in Ireland 1500–1920* (Oxford: Oxford University Press, 2001), 59, 93; and Eric Vanhaute, Richard Paping and Cormac ó Gráda, 'The European Subsistence Crisis of 1848–1850: A Comparative Perspective', in *When the Potato Failed: Causes and Effects of the 'Last' European Subsistence Crisis, 1845–1850*, eds Cormac ó Gráda, Richard Paping and Eric Vanhaute (Turnhout: Brepols, 2007), 23.

11 Charles Trevelyan, *The Irish Crisis* (London, 1848), 2 (quote); Peter Gray, *Famine, Land and Politics: British Government and Irish Society, 1843–50* (Dublin: Irish Academic Press, 1999); and David Lloyd, 'The Political Economy of the Potato', *Nineteenth-Century Contexts* 29:2–3 (2007): 311–35.

12 Redcliffe Salaman, *History and Social Influence of the Potato*, ed. J.G. Hawkes (Cambridge: Cambridge University Press, 2000 [1949]), 601–2.

13 William Cobbett, *Cottage Economy* (London, 1826), para. 80; and Ian Dyck, *William Cobbett and Rural Popular Culture* (Cambridge: Cambridge University Press, 1992).

14 Cobbett, *Cottage Economy*, para. 77, 79, 99; William Cobbett, *Cobbett's Two-Penny Trash; or, Politics for the Poor* 1 (London, 1831), 200; and Catherine Gallagher and Stephen Greenblatt, 'The Potato in the Materialist Imagination', in *Practicing New Historicism* (Chicago: University of Chicago Press, 2000), 110-35.

15 Seamus Heaney, 'Nobel Lecture: Crediting Poetry', 7 December 1995, https://www.nobelprize.org/nobel_prizes/literature/laureates/1995/heaney-lecture.html (accessed 13 April 2018).

16   Seamus Heaney, 'Digging', *Death of a Naturalist*, 1–2; 'Triptych: 1 After a Killing', *Field Work* (1979), in *Opened Ground. Poems 1966–1996* (London: Faber and Faber, 1998), 147; and 'Clearances. Sonnet 3', *The Haw Lantern* (London: Faber and Faber, 1987), 27.

17   Heaney, 'At a Potato Digging', 18–20.

18   Pablo Neruda, 'Towards an Impure Poetry', 1935, in *Pablo Neruda. Five Decades: A Selection (Poems: 1925–1970)*, ed. and trans. Ben Belitt (New York: Grove, 1974), xxi (quote); and John Dennison, *Seamus Heaney and the Adequacy of Poetry* (Oxford: Oxford University Press, 2015), 116–18.

19   David G. Anderson, Jr., 'Pablo Neruda's Noncelebratory Elementary Odes', *Romance Notes* 26:3 (1986), 226.

20   Neruda in fact wrote two odes to potatoes, one to the potato itself, and another to fried potatoes. Other odes addressed artichokes, apples, wine, maize and a very large tuna-fish that he saw in the market. Jason Wilson, *A Companion to Pablo Neruda: Evaluating Neruda's Poetry* (Woodbridge: Thamesis, 2008), 97–203 is helpful on the odes.

21   Pablo Neruda, 'Oda a la papa', *Nuevas odas elementales*, 1956, *Obras completas* (Buenos Aires: Editorial Losada, 1957), 1299–1302.

22   Adam Feinstein, 'Pablo Neruda: Experts Say Official Cause of Death "Does not Reflect Reality"', *Guardian*, 23 October 2017.

23   Yevgeny Aleksandrovich Yevtushenko, 'Epistle to Neruda', *Collected Poems, 1952–1990*, eds Albert Todd and James Ragan (New York: Henry Holt, 1991), 380; and Adam Feinstein, *Pablo Neruda: A Passion for Life* (London: Bloomsbury, 2004), 2.

Chapter 2

1 Rosalie Schweiker, personal communication, 10 October 2017.

2 Edward Terry, *A Voyage to East-India, &c.* (London, 1777), 197.

3 So are African yams (*Dioscorea*).

4 Alfred Crosby, *The Columbian Exchange: Biological and Cultural Consequences of 1492* (Westport, CT: Greenwood Press, 1972). Very recent research suggests that the sweet potato may have made its own way across the Pacific, without the help of humans: Pablo Muñoz-Rodríguez et al., 'Reconciling Conflicting Phylogenies in the Origin of Sweet Potato and Dispersal to Polynesia', *Current Biology* 28:8 (2018), 1246-56.

5 Vicente de Valverde to Charles V, Cuzco, 20 March 1539, *Cartas del Perú (1524-1543)*, ed. Raúl Porras Barrenechea (Lima: Colección de Documentos Inéditos para la Historia del Perú, 1959), 314; and 'Relación que da el Adelantado de Andagoya de las tierras y provincias que abajo se hará mención', 1545, *Pascual de Andagoya, Relación y documentos*, ed. Adrian Blázquez (Madrid: Historia 16, 1986), 138.

6 Werner König, *Dtv-Atlas zur deutschen Sprache: Tafeln und Texte mit Mundart-Karten* (Munich: Deutscher Taschenbuch, 1978), 206–7.

7 Gian Vincenzo Pinelli to Carolus Clusius, Padua, 19 September and 8 December 1597, Clusius Correspondence: A Digital edition-in-progress, ed. Esther van Gelder, http://correspondence.huygens.knaw.nl (accessed 13 April 2018).

8   Olivier de Serres, *Le theatre d'agriculture et mesnage des champs* (Paris, 1603), book 6, 513–4; and Lancelot de Casteau, *Ouverture de cuisine* (Liège, 1604), 95.

9   James McCann, *Maize and Grace: Africa's Encounter with a New World Crop, 1500–2000* (Cambridge, MA: Harvard University Press, 2005), 33–8.

10 Marx Rumpolt, *Ein new Kochbuch* (Frankfort am Main, 1581), 143b.

11 Casteau, *Ouverture de cuisine*, 95; and Wilhelm IV von Hessen to Christian I von Sachsen, Kessel, 10 March 1591, in *Quellenbuch zur sächsischen Geschichte*, ed. Paul Arras (Paderborn: Europäisscher Geschichtsverlag, 2015 [1912]), 61.

12 *Good Huswife's Jewell* (London, 1596), 20v.

13 *The Letters of John Chamberlain*, ed. Norman McClure, 2 vols (Philadelphia: American Philosophical Society, 1939), II:551; and Carolyn Nadeau, *Food Matters: Alonso Quijano's Diet and the Discourse of Food in Early Modern Spain* (Toronto: University of Toronto Press, 2016), 35.

14 Sarah Fayerweather, Manuscript cookbook, 26 June 1764, fol. 26, A/F283, Schlesinger Library, Radcliffe Institute, Harvard University, Cambridge, MA.

15 Eighteenth-Century Manuscript Recipe Book, fol. 58, MC 675, box 2, American Institute of Wine & Food Recipe Books, *c.* 1690–*c.* 1830, Schlesinger Library, Radcliffe Institute, Harvard University, Cambridge, MA.; Pierre-Joseph Buc'hoz, *Manuel alimentaire des plantes* (Paris, 1771), 485–6; and Lucas Rigaud, *Cozinheiro moderno ou nova arte de cozinha* (Lisbon, 1785), 402.

16 William Bligh, *A Voyage to the South Sea for the Purpose of Conveying the Bread-fruit Tree to the West Indies* (London,

1792), 49; and Conrad Malte-Brun, *Universal Geography, or a Description of all the Parts of the World, on a New Plan, According to the Great Natural Divisions of the Globe*, 6 vols (Edinburgh, 1822), III:551.

17 Mary Tolford Wilson, 'Americans Learn to Grow the Irish Potato', *New England Quarterly* 32:3 (1959): 336.

18 Harford Jones, *Account of the Transactions of his Majesty's Mission to the Court of Persia in the Years 1807–11*, 2 vols (London, 1834), I:429–30; and John William Kaye, *The Life and Correspondence of Major-General Sir John Malcolm*, 2 vols (London, 1856), II:46–8.

19 *Asiatic Journal and Monthly Register for British India and its Dependencies* 18 (1824): 113.

20 Minute of William Bentinck, 12 November 1803, British Library, IOR F/4/179, 5r–6r (second quote); Richard Temple, 'The Agri-Horticultural Society of India', *The Calcutta Review* 22 (1854): 341 (first quote), 342–50; and David Arnold, 'Agriculture and "Improvement" in Early Colonial India: A Pre-History', *Journal of Agrarian Change* 4:1–2: 505–25.

21 Elizabeth DeLoughrey, 'Globalizing the Routes of Breadfruit and Other Bounties', *Journal of Colonialism and Colonial History* 8:3 (2008).

22 On sailors as trendsetters see Beverly Lemire, '"Men of the World": British Mariners, Consumer Practice, and Material Culture in the Era of Global Trade, *c.* 1660–1800', *Journal of British Studies* 54:2 (2015): 288–319.

23 Kenneth Kiple, *A Moveable Feast: Ten Millennia of Food Globalization* (Cambridge: Cambridge University Press, 2007), 136. Or see Maguelonne Toussaint-Samat, *A History of Food: A New Expanded Edition*, trans. Anthea Bell (Oxford: Blackwell, 2009), 646–53.

24 See for instance Carolus Clusius to Joachim Camerarius, Frankfurt, 18 November 1589, *Clusius Correspondence*.

25 Jacques Plateau to Carolus Clusius, Tournai, 3 September 1588, *Clusius* Correspondence; Johann Royer, *Eine gute Anleitung wie man ... Garten-Gewächse ... nützen solle* (Braunschweig, 1651), 104–5; and Piotr Miodunka 'L'essor de la culture de la pomme de terre au sud de la Pologne jusqu'au mileau du XIXe siècle', *Histoire & Sociétés Rurales* 41:2 (2014): 67–84.

26 F.K. Eagle and Edward Younge, eds, *Collection of the Reports of Cases, the Statutes, and Ecclesiastical Laws Relating to Tithes*, 4 vols (London, 1826), II:228. Or see Christian Vandenbroeke, 'Cultivation and Consumption of the Potato in the 17th and 18th Century', *Acta Historiae Neerlandica* 5 (1971): 15–39; Eric Evans, *The Contentious Tithe. The Tithe Problem and English Agriculture, 1750–1850* (London: Routledge and Kegan Paul, 1976); Eloy Terrón, *España, encrucijada de culturas alimentarias: su papel en la difusión de los cultivos americanos* (Madrid: Ministerio de Agricultura, Pesca y Alimentación, Secretaría General Técnica, 1992), 143–4; and Colin Coates, *The Metamorphosis of Landscape and Community in Early Quebec* (Montreal and Kingston: McGill-Queen's University Press, 2000), 49-50.

27 James C. Scott, *The Art of Not Being Governed. An Anarchist History of Upland Southeast Asia* (New Haven: Yale University Press, 2009), 195–207.

28 See for instance Van der Ploeg, 'Potatoes and Knowledge', 209–27; Karl Zimmerer, *Changing Fortunes: Biodiversity and Peasant Livelihood in the Peruvian Andes* (Berkeley, 1996); Stephen Brush, *Farmer's Bounty: Locating Crop Diversity in the Contemporary World* (New Haven: Yale University Press, 2004); Virginia Nazarea, *Cultural Memory and Biodiversity*

(Tucson: University of Arizona Press, 2005); and Scott, *The Art of Not Being Governed*, 195–207.

29 James C. Scott, *Seeing Like a State: How Certain Schemes to Improve the Human Condition Have Failed* (New Haven: Yale University Press, 1998), 254–5.

30 Arturo Escobar, 'Power and Visibility: Development and the Invention and Management of the Third World', *Cultural Anthropology* 3:4 (1988): 428–43; and Scott, *Seeing Like a State*, 241 (quote).

31 To be precise, one person did: John Forster, *Englands Happiness Increased, or, A Sure and Easie Remedy against all Succeeding Dear Years* (London, 1664) recommended potatoes for just this reason.

Chapter 3

1 Thomas Turner, *Diary of Thomas Turner, 1754–1765*, ed. David Vaisey (Oxford: Oxford University Press, 1984), 131–2, 137; and James Stonhouse, 'Expedients for Alleviating the Distress Occasioned by the Present Dearness of Corn', *Universal Magazine* 21 (1757): 268–71.

2 These stories are collectively known as 1548 in the Aarne-Thompson-Uther Classification of Folk Tales.

3 Amanda Berry, 'Stonhouse, Sir James, Seventh and Tenth Baronet (1716–1795)', *Oxford Dictionary of National Biography*, http://www.oxforddnb.com/view/article/26582 (accessed 13 April 2018).

4 Joaquín Xavier de *Uriz, Causas prácticas de la muerte de los niños expósitos en sus primeros años*, 2 vols (Pamplona, 1801), I:6–7.

5 Andrea Rusnock, *Vital Accounts: Quantifying Health and Population in Eighteenth-Century England and France* (Cambridge: Cambridge University Press, 2002); and Yves Charbit, *The Classical Foundations of Population Thought from Plato to Quesnay* (London: Springer, 2011).

6 Bernardo Ward, *Proyecto económico, en que se proponen varias providencias, dirigidas á promover los intereses de España, con los medios y fondos necesarios para su plantificación* (Madrid, 1779), 58 (my emphasis).

7 Antoine-Augustin Parmentier, *Les pommes de terre, considérées relativement à la santé & à l'économie: ouvrage dans lequel on traite aussi du froment & du riz* (Paris, 1781), 133.

8 Jonas Hanway, *A Candid Historical Account of the Hospital for the Reception of Exposed and Deserted Young Children* (London, 1759), 10.

9 J.S. Girdler, *Observations on the Pernicious Consequences of Forestalling, Regrating, and Ingrossing* (London, 1800), 53 (quote), 88. 'That men in general should work better when they are ill fed than when they are well fed, when they are disheartened than when they are in good spirits, when they are frequently sick than when they are generally in good health, seems not very probable', observed Adam Smith: *An Inquiry into the Nature and Causes of the Wealth of Nations*, I.viii.45, *The Glasgow Edition of the Works and Correspondence of Adam Smith*, vol. 2, ed. William B. Todd (Oxford: Oxford University Press, 1975).

10 Pietro Maria Bignami, *Le patate* (Bologna, 1773), 15, 4, respectively.

11 William Buchan, *Domestic Medicine: or, a Treatise on the Prevention and Cure of Diseases by Regimen and Simple Medicines* (London, 1776), 46, 67.

12 William Buchan, *Observations Concerning the Diet of the Common People, Recommending a Method of Living Less Expensive, and More Conductive to Health, than the Present* (London, 1797), 7.

13 Rebecca Earle, 'Promoting Potatoes in Eighteenth-Century Europe', *Eighteenth-Century Studies* 51:2 (2018): 147–62.

14 Antonio Campini, *Saggi d'Agricoltura del medico Antonio Campini* (Turin, 1774), 393.

15 Food and Agriculture Organization, 'International Year of the Potato 2008', and 'Potatoes in the Kitchen', http://www.fao.org/potato-2008/en/index.html (accessed 13 April 2018).

16 M.S. Kaldy, 'Protein Yield of Various Crops as Related to Protein Value', *Economic Botany* 26:2 (1972): 142–4; and Food and Agriculture Organization, 'International Year of the Potato 2008: Potato and Water Resources', http://www.fao.org/potato-2008/en/potato/water.html (accessed 13 April 2018). A kilo of wheat is however considerably more calorific than a kilo of potatoes.

17 Massimo Livi Bacci, *A Concise History of World Population* (Oxford: Wiley, 2017), 25; and Nathan Nunn and Nancy Qian, 'The Potato's Contribution to Population and Urbanization: Evidence from a Historical Experiment', *Quarterly Journal of Economics* 126 (2011): 593–650.

18 Scott, *The Art of Not Being Governed*, 195–207; and Joram Mayshar, Omer Moav, Zvika Neeman and Luigi Pascali, 'Cereals, Appropriability and Hierarchy', http://wrap.warwick.ac.uk/82168 (accessed 13 April 2018).

19 Scott, *Seeing Like a State*; Scott, *The Art of Not Being Governed*; and James C. Scott, *Against the Grain: A Deep History of the Earliest States* (New Haven: Yale University Press, 2017), 130.

20 Trevelyan, *The Irish Crisis*, 1.

21 William Petty, *Tracts; Chiefly Relating to Ireland* (Dublin, 1769 [1672–1690]), 238, 319, 355, 366, 374.

22 Dongyu Qu and Kaiyun Xie, eds, *How the Chinese Eat Potatoes* (Hackensack, NJ: World Scientific, 2008), 23.

23 S.H. Jansky, L.P. Jin, K.Y. Xie, C.H. Xie and D.M. Spooner, 'Potato Production and Breeding in China', *Potato Research* 52:57 (2009): 57–65.

24 Xiaoping Sun, personal communication, 29 September 2017.

25 Jansky et al., 'Potato Production and Breeding in China'.

26 I owe these imaginative translations to Anne Gerritsen, Huang Lu and Claire Tang.

Chapter 4

1 'Cookery', *Times*, London, 17 February 1854, 7. The card is designed by Brainbox Candy, https://www.brainboxcandy.com/regular-sex-potatoes-greeting-card (accessed 13 April 2018).

2 Darrin McMahon, *Happiness: A History* (New York: Grove, 2006), 200. Michel Foucault, *Security, Territory, Population: Lectures at the Collège de France, 1977–1978*, ed. Michel Senellart, trans. Graham Burchell (New York: Palgrave Macmillan, 2009), 327, 338–9, is also helpful for thinking about happiness and the state.

3 Benjamin Thompson, 'An Account of an Establishment for the Poor at Munich', *Essays, Political, Economical and Philosophical*, 3 vols (London, 1797–1803), I:5.

4 Benjamin Thompson, 'Of Food, and Particularly of Feeding the Poor', *Essays, Political, Economical and Philosophical*, I:192.

5   Gallery Text, Harvard Art Museum, http://www.harvardar
     tmuseums.org/art/336163 (accessed 13 April 2018).

6   Thompson, 'Of Food', I:193–195, 202, 210–11.

7   Fritz Redlich, 'Science and Charity: Count Rumford and his
     Followers', *International Review of Social History* 16:2 (1971):
     184–216.

8   Thompson, 'Of Food', I:206–7. Sandra Sherman, *Imagining
     Poverty: Quantification and the Decline of Paternalism*
     (Columbus: Ohio State University Press, 2001) provides an
     excellent analysis of the ideology of soup.

9   Smith, *An Inquiry into the Nature and Causes of the Wealth of
     Nations*, IV.ii.4.

10   Smith, *An Inquiry into the Nature and Causes of the Wealth of
     Nations*, I.xi.39

11   *Communications to the Board of Agriculture on Subjects
     Relative to the Husbandry, and Internal Improvement, of the
     Country* 1:I-II (London, 1797), xxi.

12   Charlotte Biltekoff, *Eating Right in America: The Cultural
     Politics of Food and Health* (Durham: Duke University Press,
     2013), 50-4.

13   Martin Wainwright, 'The Battle of Rawmarsh', *Guardian*, 20
     September 2006; Richard Thaler and Cass Sunstein, *Nudge:
     Improving Decisions about Health, Wealth and Happiness*
     (New Haven: Yale University Press, 2008); *New York Times*, 2
     June 2012; 'About Us', Center for Consumer Freedom, https://
     www.consumerfreedom.com/about (accessed 13 April 2018).

14   Vincent van Gogh to Theo van Gogh, Nuenen, 30 April 1885,
     Vincent van Gogh: The Letters, http://www.vangoghletters
     .org/vg/letters/let497/letter.html (accessed 13 April 2018).
     Griselda Pollock, 'Van Gogh and the Poor Slaves: Images of

Rural Labour as Modern Art', *Art History* 11:3 (1988): 408–32 is illuminating on the painting's use of the potato to index the working-class immiseration induced by modernity.

15 John Coveney, *Food, Morals and Meaning: The Pleasure and Anxiety of Eating* (London: Routledge, 2006), 92–3.

16 Lewis Melville, *The Life of William Makepeace Thackeray*, 2 vols (London, 1899), I:261.

17 Mary Ellen Camire, Stan Kubow and Danielle Donnelly, 'Potatoes and Human Health', *Critical Reviews in Food Science and Nutrition* 49:10 (2009): 823–40; Lea Borgi, Eric B. Rimm, Walter Willett and John Forman, 'Potato Intake and Incidence of Hypertension: Results from Three Prospective US Cohort Studies', *British Medical Journal* 353:i2351 (2016).

18 Vance Thompson, *Eat and Grow Thin* (New York, 1914), 12. Brönte's dinner was a disaster. Another guest recalled that it was 'one of the dullest evenings she ever spent in her life'.

19 Biltekoff, *Eating Right in America*, 23, 33.

20 C. Fore Runge, 'Economic Consequences of the Obese', *Medscape* 56:11 (2007), 2668–72; *Healthy People=Healthy Profits* (London: Business in the Community, 2009); and 'Public Health and the US Economy', Harvard School of Public Health, 2012, https://www.hsph.harvard.edu/news/magazine/public-health-economy-election (accessed 13 April 2018).

21 Biltekoff, *Eating Right in America*, 87.

22 George W. Bush, 'Remarks on the HealthierUS Initiative in Dallas, Texas', 18 July 2003, *Public Papers of the Presidents of the United States* III: 893, The US National Archives and Records Administration, https://www.gpo.gov/fdsys/pkg/PPP-2003-book2/html/PPP-2003-book2-doc-pg889-2.htm (accessed 13 April 2018); and Biltekoff, *Eating Right in America*, 127.

23 Paul Campos, Abigail Saguy, Paul Ernsberger, Eric Oliver and Glenn Gaesser, 'The Epidemiology of Overweight and Obesity: Public Health Crisis or Moral Panic?', International Journal of Epidemiology 35:1 (2006): 58.

24 Michel Foucault, *History of Sexuality*, vol. 1: *An Introduction*, trans. Robert Hurley (New York: Pantheon, 1978), 138.

25 Foucault, *Security, Territory, Population*, 327 (quote), 338–9.

26 Georgio Agamben, *Homo Sacer: Sovereign Power and Bare Life*, trans. Daniel Heller-Roazen (Stanford: Stanford University Press, 1998).

27 Robert Crawford, 'Health as a Meaningful Social Practice', *Health: An Interdisciplinary Journal for the Social Study of Health* 10:4 (2006): 402, 416.

Chapter 5

1 Raymond Boisvert, 'Clock Time/Stomach Time', *Gastronomica* 6:2 (2006): 40–6.

2 *Gazette des beaux-arts* (Paris, 1874), 50 (quote); and Bradley Fratello, 'France Embraces Millet: The Intertwined Fates of *The Gleaners* and *The Angelus*', *Art Bulletin* 85:4 (2003): 685–701.

3 E.J. Hobsbawm and George Rudé, *Captain Swing* (Woking: Lawrence and Wishart, 1969), 15.

4 *Cobbett's Weekly Political Register*, 20 November 1830, 787; 11 December 1830; 956, 24 March 1832, 786–7; 14 April 1832, 93.

5   Girdler, *Observations on the Pernicious Consequences of Forestalling*, 67.

6   Peter Gurney, "Rejoicing in Potatoes': The Politics of Consumption in England During the 'Hungry Forties', *Past and Present* 203 (2009): 99.

7   Marilyn Strathern, 'Artifacts of History: Events and the Interpretation of Images', in *Culture and History in the Pacific*, ed. Jukka Siikala (Helsinki: Transactions of the Finnish Anthropological Society, 1990), 38 (quote); and Amiria Henare, Martin Holbraad and Sari Wastell, eds, *Thinking through Things: Theorizing Artefacts Ethnographically* (London: Routledge, 2007).

8   Nancy Ries, 'Potato Ontology: Surviving Postsocialism in Russia', *Cultural Anthropology* 24:2 (2009): 182, 202. My discussion in these paragraphs draws heavily on Ries's insights.

9   Andy Clark and David Chalmers, 'The Extended Mind', *Analysis* 58:1 (1998): 7–19.

10 *The Significance of the American Indian Institute in Indian Affairs* (Wichita: McCormick-Armstrong Press, *c.* 1923); *American Indian Institute: Wichita, Kansas* (New York: Presbyterian Church in the U.S.A. Board of Missions, 1937); and Kim Cary Warren, *The Quest for Citizenship: African American and Native American Education in Kansas, 1880–1935* (Chapel Hill: University of North Carolina Press, 2010), 159–74.

11 Janet Theophano, Eat My Words: Reading Women's Lives Through the Cookbooks They Wrote (New York: Palgrave, 2002); and Linda Murray Berzok, 'Introduction', in *Storied

Dishes. What our Family Recipes Tell Us About Who We Are and Where We've Been, ed. Linda Murray Berzok (Santa Barbara: Praeger, 2011), xvi (quote).

12 Heaney, 'Clearances. Sonnet 3', 27; Nick Kimberley, 'An Interview with Arvo Pärt and his Closest Musical Collaborators', *Gramophone*, 7 July 2016, https://www.gramophone.co.uk/feature/an-interview-with-arvo-p%C3%A4rt-and-his-closest-musical-collaborators (accessed 13 April 2018); and Karin Kopra, Arvo Pärt Centre, personal communication, 16 October 2017.

13 Leo Tolstoy, *War and Peace*, trans. Richard Pevear and Larissa Volokhonsky (New York: Vintage, 2007), 969, 972, 1020; and Richard Gustafson, *Leo Tolstoy, Resident and Stranger* (Princeton: Princeton University Press, 2014); 78–80.

INDEX

Page references for illustrations appear in italics.